BREAKING
OPEN
THE BIBLE

MAGNIFICAT®

Jean-Philippe Fabre

BREAKING
OPEN
THE BIBLE

➤ ·✴· ◄

Three simple Bible studies
to help you discover the riches of the Old
and New Testaments

Scripture excerpts from the New American Bible, revised edition.

— TABLE OF CONTENTS —

— INTRODUCTION —

You have a weekend free to discover the Bible. Or perhaps several half-days. You're on your own, in a group, or even on a retreat. Here is a very simple little companion that will help you try your hand at the Bible in those few hours.

First and foremost, the goal of these pages is to whet your appetite for reading Scripture. This little book—more a reader's guide than an encyclopedic work—makes no attempt to be exhaustive, but seeks rather to help you experience the flavor of the Bible. As you learn to read Scripture, you'll not only have a better understanding of its overall coherence, but you might also encounter passages that enlighten, nourish, and have particular meaning for you. A biblical journey always entails discoveries about oneself, about others, and about God. For some, it ends in an encounter with Christ.

How to Read the Bible

You don't have to be a Catholic to immerse yourself in this guide, but you should be aware that the principles of interpretation deployed are those of the Church. What are they?

First of all, this work is based on the conviction that one cannot read the Bible unaccompanied. The Ethiopian court official was reading from the prophet Isaiah when Philip ran up to him and asked, "Do you understand what you are reading?" "How can I, unless someone instructs me?" the Ethiopian answered (Acts 8:30-31). We need a guide to read the Bible not because the texts are complicated (though they can be), but because Scripture can only be safely interpreted from within the community that wrote it and is its steward.

Next, we need to rely on the support of those who, for centuries, have studied and interpreted the Bible. These are principally the Fathers of the Church, and their wisdom has been handed down to us as part of Sacred Tradition. Their writings contain keys to reading Scripture that continue to enrich our understanding.

Further, Catholics believe that the Scriptures are inspired writings—though written in human words, they contain the Word of God. And so, when we look for the meaning that these human authors sought to convey in their writings, we discover what God wishes to say to us. And since God chose to speak in manifold forms, we must read the various books of the Bible in close connection with each other, in a reciprocal light.

Finally, approaching the Bible according to these principles leads to an amazing insight: though ancient, these texts remain topical and stimulating today. The Bible is a true companion for every man and woman precisely because it is a living Word.

Of course, reading this little guide is no substitute for in-depth study of the Bible, though I hope it prepares you for that. Even less can it replace the liturgy, though I hope it helps you enter more fully into the Mass, which is so deeply rooted in Scripture.

Bible References

The Bible is divided into books, chapters, and verses. Each book has its own abbreviation (for example, Gn for Genesis), a list of which you should normally find at the beginning of every Bible. Then you will find the number of the chapter, followed by the verse numbers (separated by a hyphen if there are several). So, verses 42 to 50 of the ninth chapter of the Gospel of Mark is abbreviated Mk 9:42-50.

The Fathers of the Church

The Fathers of the Church lived and wrote during the first five centuries after Jesus Christ. Thinkers of the early Church, they were the first commentators on Holy Scripture, using it to clarify the Faith, to combat emerging heresies, and to establish liturgical practices. Their approach to reading the Bible has proved to be the surest method, over the centuries, of remaining faithful to Tradition. Relying on their approach also allows us to savor a particularly rich interpretation of biblical texts.

The Bible and Faith

The Bible is a "believing" book. Indeed, its human authors, writing under divine inspiration, were motivated by an act of faith. In receiving the Bible, Christians, in faith, become aware of the soundness of the teachings they have heard (Lk 1:4); thus they believe that Jesus is the Christ, the Son of God (Jn 20:31). Though a non-believer can also discover real treasures there, a full understanding of the Bible presupposes an attitude of faith.

What Is the Bible?

The Bible, as it is understood by the Catholic Church, is a library of seventy-two books. It was written over the course of a thousand years by numerous and, for the most part, anonymous authors. Some books comprise only a few pages; others are much more substantial. Regardless, Christians approach the Bible ultimately as one single volume whose seventy-two books are read in reference to one another. The Old and New Testaments, though having a certain autonomy, are read as a unified whole.

The Bible relates how God wished to make a covenant with a particular people, that they might be the sign and instrument of his divine plan: to save the world he himself had created. And so, in different forms, the authors of the Bible recount or comment on the history of the Jewish people. They make clear their conviction that this people, in its historic journey, was chosen by the one invisible God.

This divine plan finds its fulfillment in Jesus, a Jew and God's own Son. The New Testament relates and explains the life, Death, and Resurrection of Jesus, the Savior of humanity. It was to his disciples that he entrusted the interpretation of the Scriptures. They in turn set down in writing the works and message of Jesus so that generations to come might hear the Good News and conform their lives to it.

The Old and New Testaments are closely united in a relationship of promise and fulfillment. The books of the Old Testament contain the keys for the reader to fully recognize the event of Jesus Christ contained in the New. This rooting of the New in the Old underscores the historic depth of the Bible. And this depth is one of the reasons why the Bible remains topical for the reader today.

The Old and New Testaments

In the Catholic Bible, the most fundamental distinction is that made between the Old Testament—Saint Paul uses the term "old covenant" (2 Cor 3:14)—and the New Testament. The Old Testament contains the books written before the coming of Jesus Christ. The New Testament, a phrase from the Greek that can also be translated as the "new covenant," contains the books concerned with the event of Jesus Christ and its consequences.

The Scriptural Canon

It took several centuries for Christians to discern which among their writings were inspired by God. This endeavor resulted in the definition of a "scriptural canon," the list of texts that make up today's Bible. This canon was established by the Church based on criteria of antiquity, consensus, apostolic transmission, coherence with the Faith, and so forth. The content of the Bible is definitively settled for Christians, though it differs between Catholics and Protestants.

The Bible and Jesus

The Letter to the Hebrews begins: "In times past, God spoke in partial and various ways to our ancestors through the prophets; in these last days, he spoke to us through a son" (Heb 1:1-2). It would be said of Jesus that he is the plenitude of revelation, meaning that through him God spoke everything he had to say. Jesus is truly the Word of God, and it is he who gives unity to the entire Bible.

What Do We Find in the Old Testament?

The Old Testament (forty-six books) is organized into four parts:

- The Pentateuch (the *Torah*, in Jewish tradition) includes the five first and most fundamental books. The life of Moses is recounted, for the most part, in the Pentateuch.

- The historical books relate the history of Israel from its entry into the Promised Land to the period of the Maccabees (2nd century B.C.).

- The wisdom books include the psalms and the books of wisdom.

- The prophetic books include the four major and twelve minor prophets.

What Do We Find in the New Testament?

The New Testament (twenty-seven books) contains five categories of writings:

- Four books—the Gospels—are the stories of the life of Jesus, and constitute the fundamental core of the New Testament.

- The Acts of the Apostles, written by Luke, relates the life of the first Christians.

- The Pauline letters are the collected letters of Saint Paul.

- The catholic epistles ("catholic" in the sense of universal) are letters written by the apostles or persons from the apostolic age.

- Revelation, written by John, is a heavily symbolic work with many interpretations, among them that it presents a sweeping view of salvation history.

The Bible of Israel

The Hebrew Bible, that is, the Bible used by Jews to this day, contains most of the books found in our Old Testament. Jews refer to their Bible as the law (*Torah*), the prophets (*Nevi'im*), and the writings (*Ketuvim*), which give it its common name the *Tanakh*, formed by the first letters of each of these parts. They read the Bible as a prophecy of the ultimate act of salvation. For Christians, this act was the coming of Jesus Christ.

Which Translation of the Bible?

The Bible was written in Hebrew and Greek, and so most people read it in translation. In this book, we're using the translation found in the New American Bible, Revised Edition, which has been officially approved by the Church and offers several advantages: it respects the original text, it's easy to read, and it's very close to the text heard at Mass. Faithful to Tradition, it lends itself particularly well to comparisons with other biblical texts and the Fathers of the Church.

How to Use This Reader's Guide

The method is simple—it's a question of reading the Bible. This guide presents two major biblical texts in each section— an excerpt from the Old Testament and one from the New that echoes it. Along with the biblical texts, there is supporting material. The book follows the same pattern throughout, so let's take a look at how all of this unfolds.

Each of the six texts starts with an introduction—under the heading "literary context"— followed by additional information about the author and the historical and geographical context of the excerpt. This information will help us approach the biblical texts with sufficient points of reference.

Next follows the text to be studied, laid out over two consecutive left-hand pages. Short biblical quotes on the facing pages echo this text, reinforcing the fact that the Bible itself teaches us how to read the Bible, as we see how passages relate to one another. The right-hand page also contains quotes from the Church Fathers, allowing us to read the Bible in the tradition of the ancients. A series of questions, next, will help to sharpen our understanding of the Bible text we have just read. A glossary follows.

Each presentation then moves on to an explanatory commentary. The commentary is designed to help the reader savor the beauty of the biblical text, to comprehend its meaning, and to enter into personal reflection. The commentary is accompanied by short sections about such things as customs pertinent to the text, the translation, theological significance, and the spiritual message of the excerpt. A short biblical text under the heading *Lectio Divina* and a psalm for personal prayer round out the presentation.

Lectio Divina

Lectio divina, "divine reading," is a method of prayer that helps the reader enter into a passage of Scripture and discover what God reveals there. This form of biblical prayer includes the slow, reflective reading of a passage, meditation on the passage, prayer, and resting in the presence of God. Lectio divina developed within the Western monastic tradition, but it is an approach to Scripture that is accessible to all who wish to do a faith-filled reading of the texts.

What Is a Psalm?

A psalm is one of the 150 poems from the biblical Book of Psalms. *Tehillim*, the Hebrew name for the psalms, means praise, and the Book of Psalms is essentially a collection of prayers of praise as well as of supplication. Thanks to monastic tradition, they constitute the basis of Christian prayer. Jesus prayed the psalms and Christians do as well, recognizing, too, that the psalms speak about Jesus.

So now, without trepidation, let us begin our reading and together savor the biblical passages proposed in this little book.

Part One
THE SAVIOR

First Text:
The Choice of a Savior
The Birth and Youth of Moses
(Exodus 2:1-22)

—

Second Text:
The Power of Jesus
A Young Girl Restored to Life
and a Woman Healed by Jesus
(Mark 5:21-43)

In the first text, drawn from the Book of Exodus (Old Testament), Moses is prepared from his youth for his mission: to save his people from mortal peril.

In the second text, taken from the Gospel according to Saint Mark, Jesus performs acts of power: he saves two women from death.

Moses and Jesus, each in his own way, are the chosen instruments of God to save humanity.

THE CHOICE OF A SAVIOR
THE BIRTH AND YOUTH OF MOSES
(Exodus 2:1-22)

Literary context - From the Book of Genesis to the Book of Exodus

The first book of the Bible, Genesis, relates two cycles of events.

In chapters one to eleven, the biblical author narrates the story of the origins of the world. God created heaven and earth and gave them order; he placed man and woman at the center of creation and gave them dominion over it. In the first creation story, a literary gem, creation takes place over six days, at the end of which God looked at everything he had made and found it "very good" (Gn 1:31). On the seventh day, he rested (Gn 2:2).

Following a second creation account in Genesis 2, we learn that the first couple disobeyed God. Though he had forbidden them to eat from the tree of the knowledge of good and evil, they ate the fruit and forfeited the blessing with which he had crowned his creation.

Subsequent chapters recount the growing chaos into which humanity dragged the whole of creation. After Cain murdered Abel, man's depravity drove God to attempt a new beginning. He wished to renew his fallen creation. After saving Noah from the flood that deluged errant humanity, God made an eternal covenant with him and his descendants, promising that he would never again wreak such massive destruction. Yet mankind continued its works of pride, signified in the building of the tower of Babel.

How could God save men and women so enslaved by all of this? In Genesis 12 the story of the patriarchs begins and we see a new divine strategy set in place. God calls Abraham so that through him all people on earth might once again receive God's blessing. The unique election of Abraham was made with a view to the salvation of humanity. God promised Abraham descendants who would become the instrument of the liberation of all. He also promised a land for Abraham's descendants to live in. Isaac was born to Abraham in his old age, the first sign of the promise.

In the following generation, Isaac favored Jacob, his sec-ond-born son, over Esau, his firstborn. Jacob—also called Isra-el—sired twelve sons. Joseph, the youngest, was rejected by his brothers, who were jealous of him because their father favored him. They sold him into slavery and he was taken to Egypt, where he eventually became a trusted official in Pharaoh's court. During a time of famine, his brothers came to Egypt in search of food and encountered Joseph, who forgave them and who then invited them and his elderly father to settle in Egypt. The Book of Genesis culminates with the deaths of Jacob and Joseph.

The next book, Exodus, opens upon this difficult situation. The brothers are in exile and Joseph, their protector, is dead. Further, a change in scale has taken place, as the brothers' families have multiplied and became a whole people filling the land. Pharaoh, frightened by their growing numbers, punished this new people with forced labor and commanded that their male children be killed at birth. It is against this backdrop that the text we will now consider unfolds.

History - The Period of the Exodus

The historic event of the Hebrews' flight from Egypt is difficult to assess given the scant archaeological record. In general, it is thought that the Exodus took place during the nineteenth Egyptian dynasty (that of Ramses II), toward the end of the 13th century B.C.

The Author - Who Wrote Exodus?

Like the other books of the Pentateuch, Exodus was the fruit of a long process of composition whose beginning and end are hard to pinpoint. The earliest stories date from before the Babylonian exile (6th century B.C.) and perhaps go back as far as the time of David (10th century B.C.). The definitive text is a collective work incorporating earlier elements, and was probably put together sometime after the exile. The authors of Exodus are thus anonymous as well as numerous.

Geography - The Flight from Egypt

The cities of Raamses and Pithom referred to in the first chapter of Exodus were built in the Nile Delta.

THE NILE DELTA AT THE BIRTH OF MOSES

Now a man of the house of Levi married a Levite woman, and the woman conceived and bore a son. Seeing what a fine child he was, she hid him for three months. But when she could no longer hide him, she took a papyrus basket, daubed it with bitumen and pitch, and putting the child in it, placed it among the reeds on the bank of the Nile. His sister stationed herself at a distance to find out what would happen to him.

The Pharaoh's daughter came down to bathe at the Nile, while her attendants walked along the bank of the Nile. Noticing the basket among the reeds, she sent her handmaid to fetch it. On opening it, she looked, and there was a baby boy crying! She was moved with pity for him and said, "It is one of the Hebrews' children." Then his sister asked Pharaoh's daughter, "Shall I go and summon a Hebrew woman to nurse the child for you?" Pharaoh's daughter answered her, "Go." So the young woman went and called the child's own mother. Pharaoh's daughter said to her, "Take this child and nurse him for me, and I will pay your wages." So the woman took the child and nursed him. When the child grew, she brought him to Pharaoh's daughter, and he became her son. She named him Moses; for she said, "I drew him out of the water."

...

➲ Biblical Insights

Moses' basket is made with pitch, the same material used on the ark that saved Noah. The two rescues are similar.

> God said to Noah:…Make yourself an ark of gopherwood, equip the ark with various compartments, and cover it inside and out with pitch.

Genesis 6:13-14

The Letter to the Hebrews interprets the actions of Moses' parents as acts of faith, not of fear.

> By faith Moses was hidden by his parents for three months after his birth, because they saw that he was a beautiful child, and they were not afraid of the king's edict.

Hebrews 11:23

➲ Fathers of the Church

Origen compares the adoption of Moses by Pharaoh's daughter to the Church receiving the law of the Old Testament. Having had the Jewish people as nursemaid, the law came to maturity in the Church.

> I think Pharaoh's daughter can be regarded as the Church which is gathered from the Gentiles…. This, therefore, is the daughter who leaves her father's house and comes to the waters to be washed from the sins which she had contracted in her father's house. And then immediately she experiences "deeply felt compassion" and pities the child. This Church, therefore, coming from the Gentiles, finds Moses in the marsh lying cast off by his own people and exposed, and gives him out to be reared. He is reared by his own family and spends his childhood there. When, however, "he has grown stronger," he is brought to her and adopted as a son.

Origen, Homily on Exodus[1]

■■■ On one occasion, after Moses had grown up, when he had gone out to his kinsmen and witnessed their forced labor, he saw an Egyptian striking a Hebrew, one of his own kinsmen. Looking about and seeing no one, he struck down the Egyptian and hid him in the sand. The next day he went out again, and now two Hebrews were fighting! So he asked the culprit, "Why are you striking your companion?" But he replied, "Who has appointed you ruler and judge over us? Are you thinking of killing me as you killed the Egyptian?" Then Moses became afraid and thought, "The affair must certainly be known." When Pharaoh heard of the affair, he sought to kill Moses. But Moses fled from Pharaoh and went to the land of Midian. There he sat down by a well.

Now the priest of Midian had seven daughters, and they came to draw water and fill the troughs to water their father's flock. But shepherds came and drove them away. So Moses rose up in their defense and watered their flock. When they returned to their father Reuel, he said to them, "How is it you have returned so soon today?" They answered, "An Egyptian delivered us from the shepherds. He even drew water for us and watered the flock!" "Where is he?" he asked his daughters. "Why did you leave the man there? Invite him to have something to eat." Moses agreed to stay with him, and the man gave Moses his daughter Zipporah in marriage. She conceived and bore a son, whom he named Gershom; for he said, "I am a stranger residing in a foreign land."

➲ Biblical Insights

In the Acts of the Apostles, before dying a martyr's death, Stephen delivers a magnificent speech in which he takes up this episode from the life of Moses.

> When he was forty years old, he decided to visit his kinsfolk, the Israelites. When he saw one of them treated unjustly, he defended and avenged the oppressed man by striking down the Egyptian.
>
> *Acts of the Apostles 7:23-24*

Several Bible scenes take place near a well. They are always encounters between a man and a woman, like that of Jesus and the Samaritan.

> [Jesus] came to a town of Samaria called Sychar.... Jacob's well was there. Jesus, tired from his journey, sat down there at the well. It was about noon.
>
> A woman of Samaria came to draw water. Jesus said to her, "Give me a drink."
>
> *John 4:5-7*

➲ Fathers of the Church

Cyril of Alexandria compared Moses going out to his brothers to Jesus, the Word that comes from God and goes out to his brothers of the house of Israel.

> "When Moses had grown up, he went out to his brothers."... Saint Paul writes: "When the fullness of time had come, God sent his Son."... The Word thus went out to his brothers, the sons of Israel, for it is to them that belongs the promise, and he himself said: "I was sent only to the lost sheep of the house of Israel."
>
> *Cyril of Alexandria*, On Moses, Fragments[2]

Questions to Guide the Reading of the Text

Read the text carefully. If possible, read it aloud twice.

ABOUT THE BIRTH OF MOSES (page 22)

• What are the dramatic elements of his birth? Would you say that the ending of the story was foreseeable? Happy?

• What about the name of Moses? Who gave him that name? When? Is that normal? Why is this name significant?

• How many mothers does Moses have? Could we say that Moses has a double identity? Why?

• Why do you think the author recounts the birth of Moses?

ABOUT MOSES' YOUTH (page 24)

• What do we learn about Moses' personality in adulthood?

• What qualities does Moses exhibit here?

• Was it legitimate for him to kill the Egyptian? Was it legitimate for him to intervene between the two Hebrews?

ABOUT THE TEXT AS A WHOLE

• From what and how is Moses saved? In what sense does he already bear the characteristics of a savior?

• How does the narrator arouse the reader's sympathy for Moses?

• How and at what points is suspense created by the narration?

• Can you spot the irony of certain situations? What is its effect on the reader?

• If you have heard the story of Moses in the past, do you see in this excerpt elements that will be echoed in the rest of the story?

Glossary

HEBREW *(Hebrew: ivrit)*: The word used in the Bible to denote the chosen people. Its origin is uncertain. It could come from the root *avar*, meaning "to pass," or from the Egyptian *habirou*, meaning "nomad" or "vagabond."

JUDGE *(Hebrew: shephat)*: A judge in the Bible is not simply one who renders justice, but also one who governs according to the law. After entering into the Promised Land, but before a kingdom was established, Israel was governed by judges.

TRIBE: Jacob's twelve sons would give birth to the twelve tribes of Israel that bear their names: Reuben, Simeon, Levi, Judah, Dan, Naphtali, Gad, Asher, Issachar, Zebulun, Joseph, and Benjamin, as well the two semi-tribes of Ephraim and Manasseh (the sons of Joseph).

WELL *(Hebrew: beer)*: The well held a very important place in social life. Several marriages were initiated near a well (Isaac, Jacob, Moses). The word *beer* is also used in the more abstract sense of "to discover the meaning."

COMMENTARY

The authors of ancient literature typically did not spend any time chronicling the childhoods of their heroes. They concentrated instead on the hero's birth and then on his great deeds, because their goal was to reveal the person's traits and demonstrate how he had been predisposed to his mission.

The Bible does not deviate from this approach. There we find the birth of the two most important figures of the Old and New Testaments: Moses and Jesus. We've just read the finely honed account of the birth and youth of Moses, a story that, with its colloquial narration, provides keys to understanding the personality and mission of Moses.

The story of Moses is that of a saved savior. The situation was dramatic. Pharaoh had just decreed the death of all newborn Hebrew boys, God's chosen people were in mortal danger, and all of God's plan was at risk. And at that moment—a boy is born. What is to become of him? The narrator builds suspense and draws out the reader's sympathy for this beautiful baby who is the object of maternal care.

Moses' mother takes desperate action—the means she uses are highly significant. She covers a basket in pitch, just as Noah's ark was covered in pitch. This boy is saved from the water in the same way that Noah was saved from the waters of the flood. The allusion to the biblical past allows us to grasp what is at stake: the salvation of the people.

The biblical future is also being prepared. Moses is placed among the reeds as an infant; as a man he will lead his people through the Red Sea, which is also known as the Reed Sea. Moses is saved here as a foreshadowing of his people's rescue.

As the story continues, the daughter of the tyrant finds the child and, disobeying her father, decides to keep him. What irony! Pharaoh's own daughter saves a little Hebrew boy. She even has him cared for by his biological mother. Thus, a double maternity is set in place. By blood, Moses is truly a Hebrew; it is this identity that renders him sympathetic to the reader. By adoption, education, and name, he is Egyptian. His mission is being set in place. To bring his people out of Egypt he had to be fully Hebrew, yet also be capable of understanding and being integrated into the royal institutions of Egypt. The fact that he is taken for an Egyptian by the daughters of Reuel demonstrates that he was perfectly integrated within his adopted community.

In this sense, the giving of his name is interesting. The author specifies that in Hebrew this name means "drawn out of the water." This is a reference to the circumstances of Moses' birth. But ironically, this name also heralds his mission, to draw his people through the waters of the Red Sea. Pharaoh's daughter gives him this name which, in Egyptian, has a royal ring to it: the root MSS (MoSShe for Moses) can also be found in the names of pharaohs (raMSes, thutMoSe). Clearly, Moses is prepared from infancy to dialogue with the powerful.

Moses' traits are further refined, we learn, in his youth. To begin with, he is sensitive to the injustice weighing upon his people. When he sees them burdened by hard labor, he displays solidarity with them. He shows a true disposition to free his people from a state of slavery that outrages him.

We then discover his hope to settle disputes between his own people: "Why are you striking your companion?" By intervening between the two quarreling Hebrews, he displays an aptitude for governing his people. He is ready to render justice among his kinsfolk. We can see that this mission will be difficult given the reticence of even his compatriots.

At this stage of the story, however, it's not yet legitimate for Moses to act. It was illegal to kill the Egyptian and it was too soon to arbitrate between his Hebrew brothers. The culprit wasn't mistaken when he replied: "Who has appointed you ruler and judge over us? Are you thinking of killing me as you killed the Egyptian?" This episode sets up the coming chapters in which Moses will receive his double mission: to take his people's side against the Egyptians and to lead them out of Egypt. Moses' has to await God's mission orders before he can legitimately deploy his gifts for leadership.

First, however, Moses is forced to flee to Midian. This journey will take him along the route on which he will later lead his people. By making this journey for the first time on his own, Moses is in a way anticipating the flight of Israel: he learns the path to follow when fleeing from Pharaoh.

Having arrived at a well in Midian, Moses confirms his sense of justice: he defends the young women from the shepherds. This time, Moses' justice is demonstrated on behalf of people who are foreigners to him. As a symbol of Israel, Moses isn't there to free just his own people but all peoples. Reuel is not mistaken about the qualities of such a man when he asks his daughters to invite Moses to his home.

When he moves in with this foreigner, one of whose daughters he will marry, another of our hero's traits is highlighted: Moses lives as a stranger in a foreign land—thus the name he will later give his son, Gershom. This immigrant status will also be that of Israel when it settles in the Promised Land. It is part of Israel's identity to be, among nations, a nation apart.

As we see, this little story, written in such a popular style, already says much about Moses. He is progressively prepared for his mission as savior, judge, and shepherd. His double origins—Hebrew and Egyptian—will allow him to perfectly fulfill that mission. Moses will become the greatest man of the Old Testament, and the traits essential to his mission are evident from the start.

We also find mirrored here a great deal about the mission of the people of Israel. Moses is that savior who first was saved. In the same way, the people of Israel will be saved, to later become the instrument of God who wills to save all peoples. It will also be thus for Jesus, saved from the massacre of the innocents in order to consecrate himself to his mission as Savior.

Theme - One for All

The divine strategy is that of election. God chose in order to save. He not only saves those he has chosen, but also makes of his chosen ones instruments to save the greatest number. The relationship between Moses and his people illustrates this. Moses is chosen from among his people not to enjoy privilege but to receive a mission. On a different scale, this will also be the case of the people of Israel, chosen with a view to the salvation of all nations.

Customs - The Giving of a Name

In the Bible, the giving of a name completes the birth of a child. The names of biblical figures all have meaning, often linked to events surrounding their birth. The name also says something about the person, his role, or his mission. Moses is a fine example of this: the giving of his name takes place quite some time after his birth in order to show that the circumstances following his birth imbued his deepest identity. He receives the name Moses after having been "drawn out of the water."

Theology - Salvation, from Moses to Jesus

"Salvation" is the common noun derived from the verb "to save." Moses was set apart to bring salvation to his own people; he became their savior and pastor to lead them to freedom. In an analogous way, Jesus was set apart among mankind, whose cause he made his own: he is the universal shepherd, saving all people not from slavery in Egypt but from death. Theologically, it is said that Jesus came "for the salvation of the world."

Spirituality - Maternity

In contemplating the birth of Moses, we wonder at the beauty of all births. How can one be unmoved by the wombs of these two women? The biological mother, like all mothers, delights before her baby and cannot countenance the worst. The adoptive mother, moved by the baby's sobs, disobeys her own father in order to keep the child. Both of them participate in the birth of this boy who came forth from the waters of his first mother and was drawn out of the water by the second.

LECTIO DIVINA

For a meditative reading related to the birth of Moses, here are some verses from Isaiah:

But now, thus says the LORD,
  who created you, Jacob, and formed you, Israel:
Do not fear, for I have redeemed you;
  I have called you by name: you are mine.
When you pass through waters, I will be with you;
  through rivers, you shall not be swept away.
When you walk through fire, you shall not be burned,
  nor will flames consume you.
For I, the LORD, am your God,
  the Holy One of Israel, your savior.
I give Egypt as ransom for you,
  Ethiopia and Seba in exchange for you.
Because you are precious in my eyes
  and honored, and I love you,
I give people in return for you
  and nations in exchange for your life.

Isaiah 43:1-4a

PSALM FOR MEDITATION

Bless the LORD, my soul;
all my being, bless his holy name!
Bless the LORD, my soul;
and do not forget all his gifts,
Who pardons all your sins,
and heals all your ills,
Who redeems your life from the pit,
and crowns you with mercy and compassion,
Who fills your days with good things,
so your youth is renewed like the eagle's.

The LORD does righteous deeds,
brings justice to all the oppressed.
He made known his ways to Moses,
to the Israelites his deeds.
Merciful and gracious is the LORD,
slow to anger, abounding in mercy.
He will not always accuse,
and nurses no lasting anger;
He has not dealt with us as our sins merit,
nor requited us as our wrongs deserve.

For as the heavens tower over the earth,
so his mercy towers over those who fear him.
As far as the east is from the west,
so far has he removed our sins from us.
As a father has compassion on his children,
so the LORD has compassion on those who fear him.

Psalm 103:1-13

THE POWER OF JESUS
A Young Girl Restored to Life and a Woman Healed by Jesus
(Mark 5:21-43)

Part One

Literary context - Jesus' Ministry in Galilee, According to the Gospel of Saint Mark

The Gospel of Mark is one of the four Gospels in the New Testament. Each of the Evangelists has his own manner of recounting the events of the life of Jesus: they organize them according to a theological perspective rather than making them into an exhaustive chronicle. Mark was struck by the unprecedented personality of Jesus. Particularly attentive to his acts and gestures, Mark concentrates less on Jesus' teaching. The first part of his account thus sets out a series of acts revealing Jesus' power.

Unlike Matthew and Luke, Mark does not interest himself in the childhood of Jesus. Right there in the first chapter, the adult Jesus is baptized by John the Baptist. The Holy Spirit descends upon him and the voice of the Father reveals that he is the Son of God. Jesus can begin his mission. He calls his first four disciples and invites them to become fishers of men. He thus establishes a group of privileged witnesses who will remain permanently close to him.

Then, before their eyes, he begins his activities in Galilee, near the sea of the same name. For him, it is above all a question of manifesting God's benevolence through a series of healings: a man with an unclean spirit, a leper.... Certain of his acts give rise to controversy. That he forgives the sins of the paralytic and eats with sinners occasions criticism from the Pharisees, who strictly observe the law of Moses. They reproach him, accusing him of acting in the name of Beelzebub, the chief demon.

In the face of this opposition, Jesus moves on to a new stage in his ministry. He chooses eight more disciples—forming his band of twelve Apostles—and entrusts some of his powers to them. Crowds of people come to him and he speaks to them in parables. This method of instruction through enigmas encourages his listeners to question him in order to penetrate their meaning.

From then on, Jesus performs more intense signs before his disciples. They must understand who he really is and what he has come to do. He asks them to cross to the other side of the lake in a boat. During the crossing, he calms a storm, moving his disciples to wonder about his deepest identity. On the other bank, the pagan bank, he casts demons out of a possessed man. In this he demonstrates that he has come to save all people, not just the Jewish people. When he returns back to the west bank of the lake, in his own country, a long and astonishing episode unfolds, which we are now about to read. It concerns two intertwined miracles, both performed for women.

History - The Dates of Jesus' Public Ministry

Thanks to the work of biblical scholars and to elements presented in the Gospel stories, Jesus' public ministry can be dated with fairly great precision. His baptism can be dated to the start of 28 A.D. and his death most likely took place in April of the year 30. Jesus' mission lasted less than three years.

The Author - The Gospel of Mark, the First Gospel

Mark was from Jerusalem and very probably knew Jesus, though Mark was not one of the twelve Apostles. He later became a companion of Saint Paul, then of Saint Barnabas, and finally of Saint Peter. His Gospel is considered the first to have been written, and he most likely composed it while with Peter. Mark's Gospel probably served as a basis for Matthew and Luke when they wrote their Gospels. Because they follow the same general outline, the Gospels of Matthew, Mark, and Luke are called the "synoptic" Gospels.

Geography - The Sea of Galilee

The first part of Jesus' activities took place in Galilee. At the start of his public ministry, Jesus moved to Nazareth in Capernaum. This city borders the Lake of Gennesaret (also known as the Sea of Galilee) on the northwest bank.

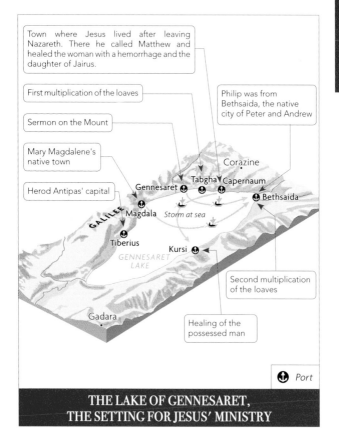

Town where Jesus lived after leaving Nazareth. There he called Matthew and healed the woman with a hemorrhage and the daughter of Jairus.

First multiplication of the loaves

Philip was from Bethsaida, the native city of Peter and Andrew

Sermon on the Mount

Mary Magdalene's native town

Herod Antipas' capital

Corazine

Tabgha Capernaum

Gennesaret

Bethsaida

GALILEE

Magdala *Storm at sea*

Tiberius

Kursi

GENNESARET LAKE

Second multiplication of the loaves

Gadara

Healing of the possessed man

Port

THE LAKE OF GENNESARET, THE SETTING FOR JESUS' MINISTRY

BIBLICAL TEXT (MARK 5:21-43)

When Jesus had crossed again [in the boat] to the other side, a large crowd gathered around him, and he stayed close to the sea. One of the synagogue officials, named Jairus, came forward. Seeing him he fell at his feet and pleaded earnestly with him, saying, "My daughter is at the point of death. Please, come lay your hands on her that she may get well and live." He went off with him, and a large crowd followed him and pressed upon him.

There was a woman afflicted with hemorrhages for twelve years. She had suffered greatly at the hands of many doctors and had spent all that she had. Yet she was not helped but only grew worse. She had heard about Jesus and came up behind him in the crowd and touched his cloak. She said, "If I but touch his clothes, I shall be cured." Immediately her flow of blood dried up. She felt in her body that she was healed of her affliction. Jesus, aware at once that power had gone out from him, turned around in the crowd and asked, "Who has touched my clothes?" But his disciples said to him, "You see how the crowd is pressing upon you, and yet you ask, 'Who touched me?'" And he looked around to see who had done it. The woman, realizing what had happened to her, approached in fear and trembling. She fell down before Jesus and told him the whole truth. He said to her, "Daughter, your faith has saved you. Go in peace and be cured of your affliction." ▪▪▪

➔ Biblical Insights

According to Jewish law, a woman with a flow of blood was unclean and it was forbidden to have contact with her. Knowing this, we can better appreciate the woman's audaciousness in approaching Jesus.

> When a woman has a flow of blood for several days...as long as she suffers this unclean flow she shall be unclean.... Anyone who touches [her] becomes unclean; that person shall wash his garments, bathe in water, and be unclean until evening.

Leviticus 15:25-27

The laying on of hands requested by the synagogue official was a means of transmitting grace or healing, as we see in the Acts of the Apostles. It became the Church's principal gesture to manifest the intervention of the Holy Spirit.

> And when Paul laid [his] hands on them, the holy Spirit came upon them, and they spoke in tongues and prophesied.

Acts of the Apostles 19:6

➔ Fathers of the Church

Hilary of Poitiers wondered at the divine power of the body of Jesus that went out from the hem of his garment. In the Bible, the garment is an extension of the person.

> The power residing in his body conferred an efficacious healing...to the frailty of [her] body in the procession of divine activity through the hem of garments.... Faith follows anywhere his power is, because it is everywhere and is absent nowhere. And the assumption of a body did not constrain the nature of his power, but his powers assumed the frailty of a body for the body's redemption, so that the operation of salvation for humanity may be contained in the hem of his garment.

Hilary of Poitiers, Commentary on Saint Matthew[3]

■■■ While he was still speaking, people from the synagogue official's house arrived and said, "Your daughter has died; why trouble the teacher any longer?" Disregarding the message that was reported, Jesus said to the synagogue official, "Do not be afraid; just have faith." He did not allow anyone to accompany him inside except Peter, James, and John, the brother of James. When they arrived at the house of the synagogue official, he caught sight of a commotion, people weeping and wailing loudly. So he went in and said to them, "Why this commotion and weeping? The child is not dead but asleep." And they ridiculed him. Then he put them all out. He took along the child's father and mother and those who were with him and entered the room where the child was. He took the child by the hand and said to her, "*Talitha koum*," which means, "Little girl, I say to you, arise!" The girl, a child of twelve, arose immediately and walked around. [At that] they were utterly astounded. He gave strict orders that no one should know this and said that she should be given something to eat.

⮕ Biblical Insights

Elijah had also invoked divine power to revive a child.

> Some time later the son of the woman, the owner of the house, fell sick, and his sickness grew more severe until he stopped breathing. So she said to Elijah, "Why have you done this to me, man of God? Have you come to me to call attention to my guilt and to kill my son?" Elijah said to her, "Give me your son." Taking him from her lap, he carried him to the upper room where he was staying, and laid him on his own bed.... The LORD heard the prayer of Elijah; the life breath returned to the child's body and he lived. Taking the child, Elijah carried him down into the house from the upper room and gave him to his mother. Elijah said, "See! Your son is alive."
>
> *I Kings 17:17-19, 22-23*

On the occasion of the raising of Lazarus, Jesus taught his disciples that for those who believe, death is no more than sleep.

> He said this, and then told them, "Our friend Lazarus is asleep, but I am going to awaken him." So the disciples said to him, "Master, if he is asleep, he will be saved." But Jesus was talking about his death, while they thought that he meant ordinary sleep.
>
> *John 11:11-13*

⮕ The Fathers of the Church

Jerome considered that the term "daughter" that Jesus uses to speak to the woman with a hemorrhage was the sign of her faith.

> She whose faith is so great deserves to be called daughter.
>
> *Jerome,* Homily 77 on Mark's Gospel[4]

Questions to Guide the Reading of the Text

Read the text carefully. If possible, read it aloud twice.

NOTICE THE INTERTWINED STRUCTURE OF THE TWO MIRACLES

- What points do these two miracles have in common?

- Why do you think they are recounted together here?

ABOUT THE RESTORATION OF THE DAUGHTER OF JAIRUS (page 42)

- In what way is Jairus' request complete?

- What is the effect produced by Jesus halting en route to take care of another healing?

- What ought to have been Jairus' reaction when told of his daughter's death?

- Why does Jesus only allow three disciples to go with him? What does he expect from these disciples, since they do not take part in the healing?

- What could Jesus really mean when he says, "The child is not dead but asleep"?

- Why do you think Jesus doesn't want the miracle to be made known?

ABOUT THE HEALING OF THE WOMAN WITH A HEMORRHAGE (page 40)

- What is the impact of such a long description of this woman's affliction?

- Whose feelings does the narrator reveal to us? What is the effect of delving into the internal thoughts of those persons? What does it tell us about them?

- Into what state does Jesus move this woman?

- We learn through Jesus that this woman has faith. What does such information inspire in the reader?

Glossary

FEAR *(Greek: phobos)*: Biblical fear denotes an attitude of pious reverence that a person experiences before God. It can, though not always, have a dimension of being afraid.

GARMENT *(Greek: himátion)*: A garment, in the Bible, is an extension of the person—so much so that a person was not allowed to keep someone else's garment as a pledge overnight. A garment can also signify the presence of the Holy Spirit, who animates the prophets (see Elijah in 2 Kgs 2:9-14).

MASTER *(Greek: didaskalos)*: In the Bible, the master is called *rabbi*. He teaches his disciples not only through words, but also through actions; the disciple becomes a follower of the master.

SEA *(Greek: thalassa)*: For theological reasons, Matthew and Mark prefer to call the Lake of Gennesaret the Sea of Galilee. The sea has a more universal dimension, but it is also more dangerous, as people can drown in its depths.

SYNAGOGUE *(Greek: sunagôgé)*: This is the building where practicing Jews gather to read and listen to the Law and the prophets. No sacrificial rites are practiced there.

COMMENTARY

Mark relates an event whose unfolding is unique in the Gospels: two miracles intertwined with each other. Unlike Matthew, Mark takes his time in recounting them. His story is very lively and his manner of narration almost vernacular. The particular arrangement of the two accounts—one story of healing with another story of resurrection—invites the reader to read these two acts of Jesus in light of each other.

A woman and a little girl are the beneficiaries of Jesus' power. Both of their biological lives are touched. The woman's loss of blood symbolizes the loss of the vital life-flow. As to the young girl, she is on the point of death. Is there any greater distress than that shared by these two? Life is ebbing away from them.

These figures, linked in their womanhood, are stricken at different points in the life cycle. Both of them share a disruption in the transmission of life: one cannot be a mother while the other cannot be a daughter. How tragic! How could a woman be unable to bear children? How could a girl not be her father's pride and joy?

Thus, through these two female figures, we are plunged into the heart of the drama of our wounded humanity. Interestingly, the woman has been afflicted for twelve years, the same age as the young girl. The woman has been barren since the girl was born. Twelve is also a number related to blessing (Jacob blessed his twelve sons, Moses blessed the twelve tribes of Israel), but here, it seems, that blessing cannot be passed on.

As we see, Mark invites a comparison between the crossed paths of these two figures who come back to life. He builds the plot by subtly playing on contrasts and similarities. Let's look at them carefully.

The contrasts in the story are numerous. First, Jesus does everything for the young girl, while he does nothing for the woman with a hemorrhage. He acts in a deliberate way to raise the girl, while a force surreptitiously goes out from him for the woman. If the girl is totally passive in her healing (the father makes the request, Jesus goes to her, her household sends news...), the woman takes all the initiative in her healing.

Then, the number of witnesses in the case of the girl keeps decreasing: Jesus separates from the crowd and only keeps three disciples with him—the designated witnesses—and he imposes silence on her family. For the woman, on the contrary, everything begins in secret before being revealed to the crowd. Finally, the miracle becomes increasingly difficult to achieve for the girl: at the start, she is still alive, then she dies. For the woman, the miracle is obtained right from the start; it is only then that the dialogue with her begins.

These contrasts invite the question of what unites the two stories. They seek to bring to light two complementary types of faith: that of the child's father and that of the woman. Both supplicants fall at Jesus' feet with a kind of fear (Jesus says to the father, "Do not be afraid," while the woman approaches Jesus "in fear"). In both miracles, it is not so much the healing that is underscored as the fact of being saved ("Come lay your hands on her that she may get well and live," "Daughter, your faith has saved you"). Finally, both are called "daughter."

While that's no surprise in the child's case, the fact that Jesus calls this adult woman "daughter" demonstrates that he is bringing her into a just filial relationship with God.

To sum up, by choosing to relate two intertwined stories, Mark provides a lesson about faith: he shows how faith in Jesus leads to life. Here, as in many other Gospel episodes, the miracle is performed in response to an approach of faith. Let's look in more detail at how Mark presents faith.

First, the Evangelist insists on faith as the overcoming of human obstacles with a view to obtaining Jesus' intervention. Jairus, the father of the young girl, must go to seek out Jesus, and wait while he heals the woman along the way; he must not become discouraged when he is told that, since his daughter is dead, it's no use bothering the master; he must not listen to those who have begun the mourning lamentations and are ridiculing Jesus. Likewise, the woman with a hemorrhage "had suffered greatly at the hands of many doctors and had spent all that she had. Yet she was not helped but only grew worse." She had to make her way through a great crowd pressing around Jesus. All these obstacles reach their peak when things become impossible in human eyes (no treatment for the woman, death for the girl).

For Mark, faith consists in believing that Jesus can act effectively when people can do nothing further. This is particularly true for Jairus. When he learns that his daughter has died, no one believes that anything more can be done: a healing, yes, that's already been seen; but to come back from the dead, no, that's impossible. The greatness of Jairus' faith is precisely that he believed that Jesus' power was boundless, extending even to the realm of death.

Faith is also believing that Jesus isn't content just to heal, but that he is capable of saving. The two requests—put into words by Jairus, kept secret by the woman—consist of begging to be saved. It's not about a simple physical benefit, of better health of body. It's really about the salvific act of drawing a person from perdition.

The two requests are addressed to Jesus as Messiah, the depositary of the Holy Spirit—the Spirit has been entrusted to him. In asking for the laying on of hands or in touching his garment (see the feature on Jesus and the Holy Spirit, page 50), the two supplicants demonstrate their high opinion of Jesus. They believe his power limitless because it is the very power of God, the Holy Spirit. What they are really asking is to be saved, that is, to receive the power of Jesus who can draw humanity back from death.

And so, in this wonderful story we learn a great deal about Jesus and the power of God. We also learn about faith, which consists in believing that Jesus is stronger than all human impossibilities.

Theme - The Miracles of Jesus

As all the Evangelists make clear, Jesus' activity is strongly characterized by miracles. But for Jesus, it is not a question of working increasing numbers of wonders. In fact, he sometimes orders that they not be made known; he is reticent when asked for such signs. Rather, Jesus has come to fulfill the salvific design of God, and it is this that he is intent on disclosing. In this context we see that miracles reveal God's benevolence toward ailing humanity. There is always a spiritual dimension to a miracle: the blind man sees the wonders of God, the deaf man hears his word, the mute proclaims his praises....

Customs - Lamentations of Mourning

Upon arriving at the home of Jairus, Jesus "caught sight of a commotion, people weeping and wailing loudly." In the East, lamentations are well-defined rites, typically performed by relatives and friends, when a person dies. The lamentations involved weeping and wailing, but also more structured songs and poems that express sorrow. These latter are set out in a literary genre called *kinah*, which the prophets also used to grieve over misfortune.

Theology - Jesus and the Holy Spirit

In this double miracle, Mark shows that Jesus is the depositary of the Holy Spirit. The synagogue official (in requesting the laying on of hands for his daughter) and the woman (by touching Jesus' garment) understood that God's Spirit was at work in Jesus. Jairus and the woman both have great faith, believing, as they do, that

Jesus has the power of the Spirit. In fact, he is called *Christ*, from the Hebrew word *messiah,* which means anointed, because he has been anointed with the Spirit to accomplish his mission.

Spirituality - The Power of Prayer

The episode of the double miracle teaches us about the power of prayer. For, indeed, both the protagonists suffer and speak to Jesus from the depths of their tribulations. Be it through a clear spoken request or by a surreptitious appeal, both approach Jesus for what they cannot obtain by themselves. Theirs are beautiful prayers, for they recognize that power emanates from Jesus. And their prayers are answered.

LECTIO DIVINA

For a meditative reading related to the prayer of the woman with a hemorrhage, here are some verses from the Gospel of Luke:

As they continued their journey [Jesus] entered a village where a woman whose name was Martha welcomed him. She had a sister named Mary [who] sat beside the Lord at his feet listening to him speak. Martha, burdened with much serving, came to him and said, "Lord, do you not care that my sister has left me by myself to do the serving? Tell her to help me." The Lord said to her in reply, "Martha, Martha, you are anxious and worried about many things. There is need of only one thing. Mary has chosen the better part and it will not be taken from her."

Luke 10:38-42

A PSALM FOR MEDITATION

My heart is stirred by a noble theme,
as I sing my ode to the king.
My tongue is the pen of a nimble scribe.

You are the most handsome of men;
fair speech has graced your lips,
for God has blessed you forever....

God, your God, has anointed you
with the oil of gladness above your fellow kings.
With myrrh, aloes, and cassia
your robes are fragrant.
From ivory-paneled palaces
stringed instruments bring you joy.
Daughters of kings are your lovely wives;
a princess arrayed in Ophir's gold
comes to stand at your right hand.

Listen, my daughter, and understand;
pay me careful heed.
Forget your people and your father's house,
that the king might desire your beauty.
He is your lord;
honor him, daughter of Tyre.
Then the richest of the people
will seek your favor with gifts.
All glorious is the king's daughter as she enters,
her raiment threaded with gold;
In embroidered apparel she is led to the king....
They are led in with glad and joyous acclaim;
they enter the palace of the king.

Psalm 45:2-3, 8b-15a, 16

Part Two:
A COVENANT OF LOVE

Third Text:
Entering into the Covenant
The Decalogue
(Deuteronomy 5:1-22)

—

Fourth Text:
Worshiping God in Spirit and in Truth
The Encounter of Jesus
and the Samaritan Woman
(John 4:3-30)

In the Book of Deuteronomy, God gives his law to the people through the intermediary of Moses. This law, which has at its heart the Ten Commandments—more precisely referred to as the Decalogue—is the sign of the covenant between God and his people.

In the Gospel of John, the Samaritan woman's encounter with Jesus leads her, from that moment, to understand that this covenant is to be lived in spirit and in truth. The new covenant, sealed by the coming of Jesus, is a law of love engraved in the hearts of men and women. It invites us to receive God's forgiveness.

— 3 —

ENTERING INTO THE COVENANT
The Decalogue
(Deuteronomy 5:1-22)

Literary context - The Flight from Egypt and the Start of Life in the Desert

After the events of his youth, Moses encounters God in the burning bush at the foot of Mount Horeb. It is there that he receives the mission to lead his people out of Egypt. For him, it means returning to seek Pharaoh's permission for the Hebrews to leave his country.

Convincing Pharoah proved extremely tough. Despite numerous signs and wonders (loosely referred to as "the plagues of Egypt"), Pharaoh remained obdurate. How could Moses make Pharaoh understand God's attachment to his elected people? Through his stubbornness, Pharaoh was putting the plan of God at risk! A final plague sent to Egypt convinced the sovereign to let the Hebrews go, but at what cost.... The firstborn of Egypt had to die in that plague before Pharaoh understood that God wished to make the Hebrew people his firstborn. Israel has never forgotten at what price God ransomed them, and commemorates this tragic liberation every year on the feast of Passover.

Thus, Pharaoh let the Hebrew people go. But then he changed his mind. And so occurred the most important event in the history of Israel: God opened a path through the sea, allowing

Part Two

the people of Israel to pass through it before engulfing the Egyptian chariots in their pursuit. The crossing of the Red Sea was the true birth of the Hebrew people. Some of the prophets considered this definitive achievement of freedom a foreshadowing of deliverance from eternal death. It is also a prophecy of the final resurrection. The people were set free.

At this point, the people found themselves in the desert, on the opposite bank of the sea. We'll now read the events that unfolded fifty days after the flight from Egypt when, on Mount Horeb, God entrusted to Moses the Decalogue, or the Ten Commandments, an instruction manual for freedom.

At this moment, God makes a covenant with his people, saying, "I will take you as my own people, and I will be your God" (Ex 6 :7). This mutual belonging is at the heart of the relationship between God and Israel. God promised to support his people. In return, the Hebrew people undertook to display godly holiness by observing the Torah (which is translated as "law"). Thus it is that the law received by Moses sets out the path of holiness.

Forty years later, in Deuteronomy, Moses once again relates this event found in the Book of Exodus. As he approached death, just as the people were about to cross the Jordan to take possession of the Promised Land, he gives the law a second time (whence comes the name *Deuteronomy*, meaning "second law"). This is the text we are now about to read.

History - Ancient Treaties

The covenant that God established with his people through the mediation of Moses can be compared to ancient treaties through which lords and their vassals made alliances. On one side, there is the promise of protection, on the other, an undertaking of fealty.

Geography - From Egypt to Canaan

Between their departure from Egypt and their entry into the Promised Land, the people received the tablets of the law on Sinai.

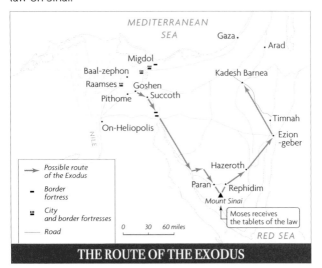

THE ROUTE OF THE EXODUS

The Author - Moses and the Pentateuch

Biblical tradition attributes the whole of the Pentateuch to Moses. Not, of course, that Moses wrote the five books with his own hand, but he is so linked to them and enjoyed such authority that they were called the "law of Moses": *Torat Moshé*. The Pentateuch closes, logically, with the death of Moses. The last of these five books, Deuteronomy, presents itself in the form of Moses' testament, even if he is not its historical author.

BIBLICAL TEXT (DEUTERONOMY 5:1-22)

Moses summoned all Israel and said to them, "Hear, O Israel, the statutes and ordinances which I proclaim in your hearing this day, that you may learn them and take care to observe them. The LORD, our God, made a covenant with us at Horeb; not with our ancestors did the LORD make this covenant, but with us, all of us who are alive here this day. Face to face, the LORD spoke with you on the mountain from the midst of the fire, while I was standing between the LORD and you at that time, to announce to you these words of the LORD, since you were afraid of the fire and would not go up the mountain:

I am the LORD your God, who brought you out of the land of Egypt, out of the house of slavery. You shall not have other gods beside me. You shall not make for yourself an idol or a likeness of anything in the heavens above or on the earth below or in the waters beneath the earth; you shall not bow down before them or serve them. For I, the LORD, your God, am a jealous God, bringing punishments for their parent's wickedness on the children of those who hate me, down to the third and fourth generation, but showing love down to the thousandth generation of those who love me and keep my commandments.

You shall not invoke the name of the LORD, your God, in vain. For the LORD will not leave unpunished anyone who invokes his name in vain. ▪▪▪

➲ Biblical Insights

The quintessence of the Decalogue is found in the following chapter of Deuteronomy, in the form of a commandment of love.

> Hear, O Israel! The LORD is our God, the LORD alone! Therefore, you shall love the LORD, your God, with your whole heart, and with your whole being, and with your whole strength. Take to heart these words which I command you today. Keep repeating them to your children. Recite them when you are at home and when you are away, when you lie down and when you get up. Bind them on your arm as a sign and let them be as a pendant on your forehead. Write them on the doorposts of your houses and on your gates.
>
> *Deuteronomy 6:4-9*

Jesus comments on the commandment regarding the sabbath, setting things in the proper order.

> The sabbath was made for man, not man for the sabbath. That is why the Son of Man is lord even of the sabbath.
>
> *Mark 2:27-28*

➲ The Targum

The Targum is a translation of the Hebrew Bible into Aramaic, with commentary. It is one of the sources that help us understand how the rabbis interpreted the Bible up until the Middle Ages. In the precept regarding parents, the repetition of the word "honor" highlights the responsibility of the children of Israel.

> My people, my people, house of Israel, be careful about the honor of your father and about the honor of your mother.
>
> *Exodus 20:12*, Targums of the Pentateuch[5]

■■■ Observe the sabbath day—keep it holy, as the LORD, your God, commanded you. Six days you may labor and do all your work, but the seventh day is a sabbath of the LORD, your God. You shall not do any work, either you, your son or your daughter, your male or female slave, your ox or donkey or any work animal, or the resident alien within your gates, so that your male and female slave may rest as you do. Remember that you too were once slaves in the land of Egypt, and the LORD, your God, brought you out from there with a strong hand and outstretched arm. That is why the LORD, your God, has commanded you to observe the sabbath day.

Honor your father and your mother, as the LORD, your God, has commanded you, that you may have a long life and that you may prosper in the land the LORD your God is giving you.

You shall not kill.

You shall not commit adultery.

You shall not steal.

You shall not bear dishonest witness against your neighbor.

You shall not covet your neighbor's wife.

You shall not desire your neighbor's house or field, his male or female slave, his ox or donkey, or anything that belongs to your neighbor.

These words the LORD spoke with a loud voice to your entire assembly on the mountain from the midst of the fire and the dense black cloud, and added no more. He inscribed them on two stone tablets and gave them to me.

⮕ Biblical Insights

The Book of Leviticus is a magisterial summing up of the second part of the Decalogue.

> You shall not hate any of your kindred in your heart. Reprove your neighbor openly so that you do not incur sin because of that person. Take no revenge and cherish no grudge against your own people. You shall love your neighbor as yourself. I am the LORD.
>
> *Leviticus 19:17-18*

In his Sermon on the Mount, Jesus comments on the Decalogue: he teaches that to speak in a hateful manner is the first step toward killing.

> You have heard that it was said to your ancestors, "You shall not kill; and whoever kills will be liable to judgment." But I say to you, whoever is angry with his brother will be liable to judgment, and whoever says to his brother, "Raqa," will be answerable to the Sanhedrin, and whoever says, "You fool," will be liable to fiery Gehenna.
>
> *Matthew 5:21-22*

⮕ Fathers of the Church

Origen elaborates on the notion of divine jealousy that we see spoken of in the Decalogue. It is not a fit of temper, but the expression of a love that wishes the salvation of mankind.

> "God is jealous": if he asks and desires that your soul cling to him, if he saves you from sin, if he reproves, if he chastises, if he is displeased, if he is angry and adopts, as it were, a certain jealousy towards you, recognize that there is hope of salvation for you.
>
> *Origen,* Commentary on Exodus[6]

Questions to Guide the Reading of the Text

Read the text carefully. If possible, read it aloud twice.

REGARDING THE CONTEXT OF THE DECALOGUE

• To whom is the Decalogue addressed?

• What is Moses' role in its transmission? Why?

STUDY THE FIRST COMMANDMENTS
(page 60)

• What is different about the first phrase ("I am the Lord....") compared to the lines that follow?

• Who are the people referred to in this verse?

• Why is the deliverance from Egypt mentioned here?

• What image of God emerges in these verses? Why does he demand such exclusivity?

STUDY THE TWO POSITIVE COMMANDMENTS
(the sabbath and honoring one's parents)

• What do these two commandments have in common?

• What do they teach us about family life?

• Why do you think they are located between the commandments regarding God and those regarding others?

STUDY THE FINAL COMMANDMENTS
("You will not commit...." to the end)

• To what area of life are these commandments directed?

• Can they all be linked? How?

HAVING STUDIED THE DECALOGUE, HOW WOULD YOU SUM IT UP AS A WHOLE?

Glossary

COVENANT *(Hebrew: berit)*: The covenant was a mutual commitment between God and his people. The Sinai covenant is the most fundamental one of the Old Testament. Jesus came to seal the new and final covenant, which fulfilled the first.

HOREB: Located in the heights of Sinai, Horeb is called the "mountain of God." It is here that God concluded his covenant with Moses.

MERCY *(Hebrew: hesed)*: A complex biblical word that denotes a relationship between goodness and love, and implies a faithful and profound affection. The psalms use this word to speak of the goodness of God toward humanity.

SABBATH: The seventh day of the week. In the creation story, it was the day when God ceased his work of creation (Gn 2:2-3) and rested. Reminded of the divine rest, and of the freedom God grants, the people of the first covenant observed the sabbath.

WORD *(Hebrew: dabar)*: The term denotes an effective word and thus, by extension, can also signify a thing, an event, a revelation. It is also the root of the word for "desert" (*midbar*), the place where God speaks.

COMMENTARY

The Decalogue is at the heart of the faith of Israel. In the Pentateuch as a whole—the Torah—we find 613 commandments. The ten that Moses brought down from the mountain on the tablets constitute the kernel. All the other commandments, in one form or another, are contained within this Decalogue.

There are two similar versions of the Decalogue: the one that appears in Exodus recounts the events on Mount Horeb at the time; the other, in Deuteronomy, situates the episode forty years later when Moses, before his death, leaves his testament. It is the second that we are studying here.

The first verses are interesting, for they set the scene of the action in a significant way. In them we learn three important elements that orient the receiving of the Decalogue.

First of all, Moses specifies who the covenant is destined for: "Not with our ancestors did the Lord make this covenant, but with us, all of us who are alive here this day." Even forty years after Horeb, when the preceding generation had passed away, the Decalogue remained topical. By being valid "here this day," the Decalogue is valid always and everywhere. This is a narrative device to assert its perpetual validity.

Then, Moses indicates his own role: "I was standing between the Lord and you." Moses serves as mediator between God and the people. Divine revelation is delivered through human mediation. When God speaks, he uses men and women as instruments of his word. This is a constant in biblical history. It will be the role of the prophets and, in a perfect manner, of Jesus.

Finally, nearly the last words that occur before the Decalogue itself are: "the Lord spoke." Not "he commanded," or "he demanded," or "he decreed." In English, we commonly refer to the Ten "Commandments." This is incorrect or, at least, only an approximation. The Jewish Bible speaks of ten "words." This is why the translation "Decalogue" is preferable. Indeed, God here gives ten words that are not constraints, but, rather, form an instruction manual for freedom.

Let us now enter into the Decalogue itself. A surprise awaits us, for the first word is not an injunction but an introduction: "I am the LORD your God, who brought you out of the land of Egypt, out of the house of slavery." The Lord introduces himself in a guise that will mark all that follows: he defines himself as a liberator God who has freed his people. He did not liberate them from one slavery, however, just so they could enter another. The words of the Decalogue are the words of a God who wishes humanity to be free.

And yet almost all of the injunctions that follow are negatives! "You shall not have other gods beside me. You shall not make for yourself an idol.... You shall not invoke the name...." Is this really compatible with freedom? At first sight, certainly not. But upon careful reflection, we understand that God is alerting us to areas of non-life, and thus of non-freedom. It's a bit like a mother telling her child, "You shall not stick your fingers in the electric socket." Until the child is able to know this for himself, the law enables him to grow up. What is signposted here is the zone outside of which any life, and thus any freedom, is impossible.

We do not have space here to develop the interpretation of the first injunctions. We may simply remark that they all concern the relationship with God. They are what is commonly referred to as the first tablet of the law. We find in it a strong insistence on the question of the image of God. He who makes an image of God reduces him to his own conceptions. But God is always greater than anything we can conceive of. To be the people of the covenant is to renounce all images of God in order to enter into a relationship of trust, of faith.

Then come two central injunctions that have several points in common: "Observe the sabbath day—keep it holy" and "Honor your father and your mother." Both are positive statements exhorting us to behave according to God's order. Above all, they both concern the family sphere. For in the injunction about the sabbath, parents must prove themselves good parents by freeing their children from work on that day, as God did by freeing his people. In the injunction about parents, it is the child who must be a good child by honoring those who gave him life. In all of this, the father's behavior must be in the image of the heavenly Father to make it understood that God wishes to free his children. In return, children must understand that, through their parents, all life comes from God. In honoring them, they recognize God's paternity.

We see here what importance the Bible places on the family as the school of apprenticeship in a just relationship with God. It is in the family that the transmission of the law of God plays out. We also find the same in the *Shema Yisrael* text (Dt 6:4-9, see page 61). The two positive family injunctions are the hinge between the requirements toward God and those toward others. For it is in the heart of the family that a child learns that he is also a child of God.

The last injunctions, called the second tablet, are commonly referred to as the commandments regarding one's neighbor. Yet when you look at them carefully, they are more about respect for life, in that it is sacred. In saying "You shall not kill," God calls for respect of biological life. People cannot restore life once they have taken it. In saying "You shall not commit adultery," God calls for respect of the sanctuary of life that is the family. This sanctuary is sacred precisely because it is there that life is transmitted. Finally, in saying "You shall not steal," God calls for respect for the means of subsistence. He who steals a water gourd in the desert endangers the life of another.

These three realms of respect for life are continued in the three final injunctions that flow from them. "To bear dishonest witness against your neighbor" can lead to his murder, through an unjust death sentence. To "covet your neighbor's wife" leads to adultery, and to covet "anything that belongs to him" leads to stealing. And so the Decalogue is not satisfied with putting us on our guard against the externals of our acts, but warns us about the attitudes that influence our actions, notably covetousness.

We now better understand why the Decalogue allows us to knit a more just relationship with our Creator and, following from that, with other creatures. The Decalogue is truly an education in freedom and a pathway of life.

Part Two

Theme - The Torah

The term Torah comes from a Hebrew verb rich in meaning: *yarah*, meaning "to throw far away," "to raise one's hand," "to point in a direction." In the Bible, it takes on a metaphorical sense, that of the direction to follow in life. It is thus the whole of the instructions that God gives to show us the right direction to take, the path that allows us to live an upright life. Based on this, the Greek translates Torah as *nomos*, "law." Later, the first five books of the Bible, called the Pentateuch in Greek, were given the name Torah. It is a word very closely associated with the person of Moses, who received the Torah on the mountain.

Customs - The Tabernacle

When Moses went up the mountain he received, among other things, the plans of the "tabernacle," which means the "meeting tent." This was a mobile sanctuary that held the ark of the covenant—the chest housing the tablets of the law. God manifested his presence by a cloud at the entrance of the tent enclosing the ark. The tabernacle moved with the people through the desert until the ark of the covenant reached Jerusalem, where the definitive permanent tabernacle was to be built: the Temple.

Theology - The Law and Faith

In several of his epistles (e.g., Romans, Galatians), Saint Paul insists on the respective roles of the law and faith. The law aims at enlightening our conscience by helping us discern the difference between good and bad actions. It enables us to recognize that we are sinners. Yet the observance of the law cannot save us, for we cannot raise ourselves up to God through our own efforts. Faith in Jesus Christ alone saves us, for Jesus gives his grace to those who recognize him as the Savior.

Spirituality

The term "examination of conscience" refers to a spiritual practice that can be performed at any time but is used most often in preparation for attending Mass, for receiving the Sacrament of Reconciliation, and at the end of each day. It consists of reviewing your actions and thoughts in light of the Word of God with the intent of noting where you have done well and where you have sinned. The Decalogue exhaustively covers all realms of human behavior, before God and before our neighbor, and is a good place to start when examining your conscience.

LECTIO DIVINA

For a meditative reading related to the Decalogue, here are some verses from the Gospel according to Matthew:

When the Pharisees heard that he had silenced the Sadducees, they gathered together, and one of them [a scholar of the law] tested him by asking, "Teacher, which commandment in the law is the greatest?" He said to him, "You shall love the Lord, your God, with all your heart, with all your soul, and with all your mind. This is the greatest and the first commandment. The second is like it: You shall love your neighbor as yourself. The whole law and the prophets depend on these two commandments."

Matthew 22:34-40

A PSALM FOR MEDITATION

Blessed those whose way is blameless,
who walk by the law of the LORD.
Blessed those who keep his testimonies,
who seek him with all their heart.
They do no wrong;
they walk in his ways.
You have given them the command
to observe your precepts with care.
May my ways be firm
in the observance of your statutes!
Then I will not be ashamed
to ponder all your commandments.
I will praise you with sincere heart
as I study your righteous judgments.
I will observe your statutes;
do not leave me all alone.

Be kind to your servant that I may live,
that I may keep your word.
Open my eyes to see clearly
the wonders of your law.
I am a sojourner in the land;
do not hide your commandments from me.
At all times my soul is stirred
with longing for your judgments.
With a curse you rebuke the proud
who stray from your commandments.
Free me from disgrace and contempt,
for I keep your testimonies.

Psalm 119:1-8, 17-22

Part Two

— 4 —

WORSHIPING GOD IN SPIRIT AND TRUTH

The Encounter of Jesus and the Samaritan Woman

(John 4:3-30)

Literary context - The Encounters of Jesus in the Gospel of John

The Gospel of John is also called the fourth Gospel. Indeed, John was the last of the four Evangelists to write (at the very end of the 1st century), and his work figures last in the biblical ordering of the Gospels.

The specificity of his writing sets him apart from the other three. John doesn't follow the same outline and doesn't recount the same episodes as Matthew, Mark, and Luke, though he, of course, concludes like all the others with the cycle of the Passion and Resurrection. But his manner of approaching the public ministry of Jesus is very different. He chooses fewer episodes and spends more time unfolding them. In the conclusion before his epilogue he says: "These are written that you may [come to] believe that Jesus is the Messiah, the Son of God, and that through this belief you may have life in his name" (Jn 20:31).

Using a smaller vocabulary than the others, John favors a more symbolic reading without being any less historical. He organizes his Gospel like a great trial in which a succession of people, representing different aspects of humanity, enter the witness stand. These figures are called to take a position regarding the One who is accused through the malice of men.

Chapter 1 opens with the figure of John the Baptist, the first to position himself in relation to Jesus. It is he who points Jesus out to his own disciples: "Behold, the Lamb of God." On the strength of this, they go to see where Jesus is staying, and come to believe that they have found the Messiah. They then decide to speak of him to others and to follow him. As early as chapter 2, they are present at the first signs performed by Jesus: the water turned into wine at the wedding at Cana and the cleansing of the Temple in Jerusalem.

Then begins a succession of long dialogues that sometimes spread over a whole chapter: the nocturnal meeting of Jesus and Nicodemus (Jn 3), and his encounter with the Samaritan woman (Jn 4), which we are going to read. These two encounters essentially unfold in private. They reveal the art with which Jesus prompts the person with whom he speaks—and the reader as well—to self-knowledge and an understanding of the divine mystery.

When Jesus begins his healings, his encounters become the subject of lively debate: this is the case for the healing of the paralytic at the pool called Bethesda on the day of sabbath rest (Jn 5), and the healing of the man born blind, whom he sends to the Pool of Siloam (Jn 9). The opposition of the Jewish authorities reaches its apex when Jesus raises Lazarus from the tomb (Jn 11).

As you read one of these encounters, that with the Samaritan woman, let John's style, with its finely honed dialogue, carry you along on a spiritual journey.

History - Samaria and the Jews

Samaria is a region situated between Judea, to the south, and Galilee, to the north. Through the ebb and flow of a devastating almost thousand-year history, the Jews and the Samaritans had become enemy brothers: the Samaritans did not worship in Jerusalem but on Mount Gerizim, and their Bible was restricted to the Torah.

The Author - John, the Beloved Disciple

Christian tradition identifies the apostle John as "the disciple whom Jesus loved" referred to in the Gospel. Accordingly, the work highlights the warmth between this disciple and Jesus. The conclusion of the Gospel specifies that "it is this disciple who testifies to these things and has written them" (Jn 21:24).

Geography - Geopolitical Palestine of the 1ˢᵗ century

In the time of Jesus, Palestine was part of the Roman province of Syria and was called Judea. It was divided into four parts: Galilee, under the tetrarchy of Herod Antipas; to the north, the tetrarchy of Philip; the Decapolis to the west; and Judea-Samaria, under the authority of the procurator Pilate.

MEDITERRANEAN
SEA

GAULANITIS

GALILEE

DECAPOLIS

SAMARIA

PEREA

Jérusalem .

JUDEA

Tetrarchy of Herod Antipas
Roman province (Pilate)
Tetrarchy of Philip

0   15   30 miles

PALESTINE IN THE 1ST CENTURY

[Jesus] left Judea and returned to Galilee.

He had to pass through Samaria. So he came to a town of Samaria called Sychar, near the plot of land that Jacob had given to his son Joseph. Jacob's well was there. Jesus, tired from his journey, sat down there at the well. It was about noon.

A woman of Samaria came to draw water. Jesus said to her, "Give me a drink." His disciples had gone into the town to buy food. The Samaritan woman said to him, "How can you, a Jew, ask me, a Samaritan woman, for a drink?" (For Jews use nothing in common with Samaritans.) Jesus answered and said to her, "If you knew the gift of God and who is saying to you, 'Give me a drink,' you would have asked him and he would have given you living water." [The woman] said to him, "Sir, you do not even have a bucket and the well is deep; where then can you get this living water? Are you greater than our father Jacob, who gave us this well and drank from it himself with his children and his flocks?" Jesus answered and said to her, "Everyone who drinks this water will be thirsty again; but whoever drinks the water I shall give will never thirst; the water I shall give will become in him a spring of water welling up to eternal life." The woman said to him, "Sir, give me this water, so that I may not be thirsty or have to keep coming here to draw water." ■■■

➲ Biblical Insights

As we have already seen with Moses (pages 19-35), many encounters take place near a well. They very often involve a man and a woman, and end in marriage.

> The young woman was very beautiful, a virgin, untouched by man. She went down to the spring and filled her jug. As she came up, the servant ran toward her and said, "Please give me a sip of water from your jug." "Drink, sir," she replied, and quickly lowering the jug into her hand, she gave him a drink.

Genesis 24:16-18

Luke recounts other scenes illustrating the difficulties between Samaritans and Jews.

> [Jesus] sent messengers ahead of him. On the way they entered a Samaritan village to prepare for his reception there, but they would not welcome him because the destination of his journey was Jerusalem.

Luke 9:52-53

➲ The Fathers of the Church

John Chrysostom astutely compared the Samaritan woman to Nicodemus, with whom Jesus had spoken in the previous chapter: he underscores the progression between the two.

> Peaceful and mild, in the noonday sun, the Samaritan woman listens and responds. She perseveres until she gets what she was looking for. The woman straightway believed, showing herself much wiser than Nicodemus, and not only wiser, but more manly. For he when he heard ten thousand such things neither invited any others to this hearing, nor himself spoke forth openly; but she exhibited the actions of an Apostle.

Saint John Chrysostom, Commentary on John[7]

■■■ Jesus said to her, "Go call your husband and come back." The woman answered and said to him, "I do not have a husband." Jesus answered her, "You are right in saying, 'I do not have a husband.' For you have had five husbands, and the one you have now is not your husband. What you have said is true." The woman said to him, "Sir, I can see that you are a prophet. Our ancestors worshiped on this mountain; but you people say that the place to worship is in Jerusalem." Jesus said to her, "Believe me, woman, the hour is coming when you will worship the Father neither on this mountain nor in Jerusalem. You people worship what you do not understand; we worship what we understand, because salvation is from the Jews. But the hour is coming, and is now here, when true worshipers will worship the Father in Spirit and truth; and indeed the Father seeks such people to worship him. God is Spirit, and those who worship him must worship in Spirit and truth." The woman said to him, "I know that the Messiah is coming, the one called the Anointed; when he comes, he will tell us everything." Jesus said to her, "I am he, the one who is speaking with you."

At that moment his disciples returned, and were amazed that he was talking with a woman, but still no one said, "What are you looking for?" or "Why are you talking with her?" The woman left her water jar and went into the town and said to the people, "Come see a man who told me everything I have done. Could he possibly be the Messiah?" They went out of the town and came to him.

➲ Biblical insights

Through the voice of the prophet Jeremiah, God compares himself to a source of living water abandoned by the people.

> Two evils my people have done:
>> they have forsaken me, the source of living waters;
>
> They have dug themselves cisterns,
>> broken cisterns that cannot hold water.

Jeremiah 2:13

The Second Book of Kings deplores the growing number of shrines in Samaria, which would lead to idolatry and an increase in the number of divinities.

> Thus each of these nations continued to make its own gods, setting them up in the shrines of the high places the Samaritans had made: each nation in the cities in which they dwelt.

2 Kings 17:29

➲ The Fathers of the Church

Saint Cyril beautifully comments on the journey this woman makes.

> The woman who, two or three days ago, had many men now shows herself to be stronger and superior to the cares of the flesh. And she who was often easily caught by illusory pleasures reaches beyond the so-called necessities of the flesh, disregarding both thirst and drink, and is forged anew into another disposition through faith. Immediately, she exercises love, the fairest virtue of all and the way of affection for others. She runs into the city, quickly announcing to the others the blessing that she had found. The Savior was echoing within her, at least so it seems, and whispering secretly in her mind, saying, "Freely you have received, freely give."

Cyril of Alexandria, Commentary on John[8]

Questions to Guide the Reading of the Text

Read the text carefully. If possible, read it aloud twice.

COMPARE THE EPISODE OF THE SAMARITAN WOMAN (page 78) WITH MOSES' ENCOUNTER AT THE WELL (page 24)

• What are the common points in the succession of events?

• How does the episode with Moses end?

• How do each of the two episodes broach the question of marriage?

BE ATTENTIVE TO THE SETTING OF THE DIALOGUE

• What might the geopolitical and religious setting of Samaria represent?

• Is it normal for a woman to come to fetch water at noon? In this story, what might explain the time of day?

BE ATTENTIVE TO THE DEVELOPMENT OF THE DIALOGUE

• Who takes the initiative in the conversation?

• What are the important stages? You might write down an outline of the story, highlighting its pivotal moments.

• How does Jesus manage to move the woman forward?

• What does the Samaritan woman learn about herself? About Jesus?

READ THE DIALOGUE FROM A PERSONAL PERSPECTIVE

• In what ways do you identify with the Samaritan woman?

• What does this story teach you about Jesus' way of going about things?

• Is there an element that you particularly enjoyed in this Gospel reading?

Glossary

——— ➤ ☀ ◆ ———

JEW *(Greek: ioudaios)*: The name the Romans gave the inhabitants of Judea, the region covering principally the ancient territory of the tribe of Judah. By extension, it was the name given to all those following the religion of Israel.

MESSIAH *(Greek: christos)*: The Hebraic root word (*messiah*) and the Greek root (*christos*) refer to the same thing: the anointed of the Lord. In the Old Testament, kings, prophets, and priests had all been anointed, but one was awaited who would be anointed par excellence: the Christ, or Messiah. Christians recognize him in Jesus Christ, anointed with the Holy Spirit.

PROPHET *(Greek: prophétès)*: One who speaks on behalf of God. A prophet received the divine mission to call people to conversion and to interpret events. Many prophets are recognized in the Old Testament. John the Baptist was the last prophet of Israel. Jesus is likened to a prophet, but is more.

SALVATION *(Greek: sôtéria)*: A common noun derived from the verb "to save." It denotes both the act of saving and that of being saved.

WORSHIP *(Greek: proskuneô)*: Literally, this verb means "to bow down." This was the posture adopted before God in recognition of his grandeur, in the relationship of creature to Creator.

COMMENTARY

The meeting of Jesus with the Samaritan woman is the setting for one of the most beautiful dialogues of the Gospel. With incomparable delicacy, Jesus prompts this foreign woman to an authentic encounter with him.

To fully savor this passage, we must understand the circumstances. By voluntarily passing through Samaria, a territory normally avoided by Jews, Jesus provokes a very unexpected encounter. All the odds were against such a meeting, a fact the narrator emphasizes by pointing out the improbable circumstances: that Jesus remained alone, that a man would address a woman, that a Jew would speak to a Samaritan—all elements that make this conversation as improbable as it is risky.

Bible readers that we are, we are immediately struck by the similarities to the episode of Moses at the well (page 24). There are numerous scenes of this type in the Old Testament (see the Customs feature, page 88). Each time, in these stories, a man is waiting by a well, a woman arrives, water is given, and a conversation ensues. Finally, the woman returns home and things end in marriage. Saint John, without doubt, relied on these encounters at a well for his model: he uses the same scenario, though the encounter here does not end in marriage. Yet the theme of marriage is broached by Jesus. We must bear this in mind.

Let's go back to the beginning of the dialogue in order to understand the structure of the teaching method that Jesus is setting in place. It can be broken down into seven stages.

❶ Jesus expresses a need. He begins by asking for water. Rather than proposing to give, he asks to receive. He puts himself in the position of a beggar. He, the Lord, does not impose himself from on high. He makes himself humble: he admits a need. He thus makes clear that he wants the collaboration of this woman and her commitment. The woman is surprised by such a request in which we've already sensed all the incongruity.

❷ Jesus arouses curiosity. He prompts the woman a step further by saying to her: "If you knew the gift of God and who is saying to you, 'Give me a drink....'" With great delicacy, he allows her to work out that there is in him something greater than she could have suspected. He invites her to consider a role reversal: who is it that really needs the other? Isn't it the woman who should have been asking him for a drink? Then Jesus tells her that he is ready to give. All are so many ways of prompting this woman to ask herself about the identity of this man! "Are you greater than our father Jacob?"

❸ Jesus steers her toward heavenly realities. Having spurred the woman to active curiosity, he can reveal to her what he wishes to give her: water that truly quenches thirst. He seeks to lead this woman from material to spiritual interests. He doesn't hesitate to open up perspectives of eternal life to her. By revealing a higher level of life, he arouses her thirst for this new water. And yet, the Samaritan woman's quest is still marked by material concerns: she desires this water so that she doesn't "have to keep coming here to draw water."

❹ Jesus spurs her to see the truth of her life. Having aroused in her a thirst for meaning, Jesus changes the subject and questions the woman about her conjugal life. He leads her to recognize that her life is disordered (we deduce that her shame is the reason she goes to the well when no one else is there), but he doesn't condemn her. The woman, seeing Jesus' wisdom in the domestic domain, questions him about the religious domain. She senses that there's a link between faithfulness to her husband and faithfulness to God. Thus she takes a further step toward setting her life in order. At the same time, she grows in her recognition of Jesus, in whom she discerns a prophet.

❺ Jesus guides her to true worship. He prompts the woman to a true encounter with God. In saying to her, "The hour is coming, and is now here, when true worshipers will worship the Father in Spirit and truth," he steers her toward a just relationship with God. Jesus has not drawn the woman to himself but to the Father. In addition, he reminds her *how* to encounter God, since salvation comes from the Jews. It is precisely that which drives the woman to question him about the Messiah.

❻ Jesus reveals his identity. The woman acknowledges that the Messiah is coming and Jesus, taking this opening in the conversation, finally states that he is the Messiah. He does so without even having to repeat his own title: "I am he, the one who is speaking with you." And that's that: Jesus' identity is fully revealed.

Now we must return to the question of marriage that we left hanging earlier. In biblical tradition, the Messiah was expected to come as the spouse of his people (see the Theme feature, page 88). John had already recounted the wedding at Cana (Jn 2:1-12) so that it would be understood that Jesus is the true spouse of the wedding with humanity. Although the episode of the Samaritan woman does not culminate in a marriage, one can say that Jesus is the true spouse, he who comes to fulfill the desire of every human soul (see the Spirituality feature, page 89).

❼ The woman proclaims Jesus. The Samaritan woman's journey does not, however, end on this high point of the encounter. When the disciples arrive, the woman returns to the town. It is a nice touch that this encounter ends in Jesus' absence. Over the course of her encounter with Jesus, the Samaritan woman has acquired a certain autonomy. She is capable of speaking about him in his absence, which she in her turn does with great delicacy. She doesn't speak in his place, but invites others to meet Jesus themselves. Her words "Could he possibly be the Messiah?" indicate Jesus' identity, but she doesn't force it on them. Her question invites each one of them to consider and recognize Christ for him or herself. In this, the woman has become a missionary witness to Jesus.

Had we continued reading in the text, we would have learned that Jesus stayed with the Samaritans for two days, and growing numbers of the townspeople came to believe through hearing his own words. They tell the Samaritan woman: "We no longer believe because of your word; for we have heard for ourselves, and we know that this is truly the savior of the world." The woman effaced herself before Jesus.

This dialogue reveals what the new covenant is: Not a mutual engagement based on the observance of a law (the woman would have been condemned under the law of Moses), but a reciprocal commitment in a relationship of love in which Jesus comes to save sinful humanity and lead it toward true worship.

Theme - Nuptials

The theme of nuptials is best developed in the Old Testament by the prophet Hosea. He speaks of the covenant God made with his people in terms of a wedding. It was considered an indissoluble and faithful commitment. God loves his people like a bridegroom and he speaks to their heart. This metaphor of marriage allows us to go beyond an overly legalistic concept of the covenant established on Sinai, when Moses received the gift of the law. In the New Testament, Jesus acknowledges himself the true spouse of the Church.

Customs - Wells and Marriage

Isaac's servant finds a wife for his master near a well (Gn 24:10-14). Jacob, too, meets his wife Rachel sitting at a well (Gn 29:9-14). The same is true for Moses in the episode we read in the first cycle (Ex 2:15-22, see pages 19-35). All of these episodes, in which water is drawn and shared, end in marriage. So it's natural that Jesus should question the Samaritan woman about her married life.

Theology - A Catechumen's Journey

Since the beginning of the Church, people have prepared to be baptized at the Easter Vigil. The time of preparation has always included Lent (the six weeks before Easter), but has been stretched out over several years at various times in Church history. Those being prepared are called catechumens and their period of instruction is known as the catechumenate. During the six Sundays of Lent, those on this spiritual journey toward baptism hear some of the great stories from the Gospel of John. The first of these is the dialogue with the Samaritan woman. It's easy to see why, for this dialogue highlights the tact with which Jesus leads each of us to knowledge of him.

Spirituality - Jesus and the Human Soul

Many of the Church Fathers read the story of the Samaritan woman as a metaphor for the encounter between Jesus and every human soul. Jesus approaches everyone with respect for their profound freedom: through a dialogue in which he progressively reveals himself, he allows all who encounter him to judge for themselves the truth about his own being.

LECTIO DIVINA

For a meditative reading related to the encounter with the Samaritan woman, here are some verses from the Prophet Isaiah:

On that day, you will say:
I give you thanks, O Lord;
   though you have been angry with me,
   your anger has abated, and you have consoled me.
God indeed is my salvation;
   I am confident and unafraid.
For the Lord is my strength and my might,
   and he has been my salvation.
With joy you will draw water
   from the fountains of salvation,
And you will say on that day:
   give thanks to the Lord, acclaim his name;
Among the nations make known his deeds,
   proclaim how exalted is his name.
Sing praise to the Lord for has done glorious things;
   let this be known throughout all the earth.
Shout with exultation, City of Zion,
   for great in your midst
   is the Holy One of Israel!

Isaiah 12:1-6

A PSALM FOR MEDITATION

Glorify the LORD, Jerusalem;
Zion, offer praise to your God,
For he has strengthened the bars of your gates,
blessed your children within you.
He brings peace to your borders,
and satisfies you with finest wheat.
He sends his command to earth;
his word runs swiftly!
Thus he makes the snow like wool,
and spreads the frost like ash;
He disperses hail like crumbs.
Who can withstand his cold?
Yet when again he issues his command, it melts them;
he raises his winds and the waters flow.
He proclaims his word to Jacob,
his statutes and laws to Israel.
He has not done this for any other nation;
of such laws they know nothing.
Hallelujah!

Psalm 147:12-20

Part Three:
THE PRESENCE OF GOD

Fifth Text:
What Dwelling for God?
The Oracle of Nathan
(2 Samuel 7:1-22)

—

Sixth Text:
Recognizing the Risen One
The Disciples of Emmaus
(Luke 24:13-35)

In the Second Book of Samuel, David understands that it is not for him to build the Temple of God. It is God who chooses how he is to dwell among men: he will live in a house made of stone, but also in the descendants of David.

At the end of Luke's Gospel, after the Resurrection, Jesus will make himself known to the disciples of Emmaus as a God present in a radically new way and yet in conformity with Scripture.

— 5 —

WHAT DWELLING FOR GOD?
The Oracle of Nathan
(2 Samuel 7:1-22)

Literary context - David's Accession to the Throne

The First Book of Samuel tells the story of Saul, the first king of Israel. His reign took place after the period of the judges, who had governed Israel for over two hundred years following the death of Moses and the people's entrance into the Promised Land. Saul was anointed by Samuel, but Saul lost God's favor and God soon rejected him. It was then that God singled David out to be secretly anointed by Samuel with royal unction to become the future king.

At the beginning of Saul's reign, David was in favor with the king, notably because David, in killing the powerful Goliath, had freed the people from the Philistine threat. Saul gave him his own daughter, Michal, in marriage, but he was jealous of David and wanted to eliminate him. David owed his life to Saul's son, Jonathan, who warned him of Saul's intention so that David was able to make his escape. He then began a nomadic life at the head of a band of men, but Saul set off in pursuit. Several times, David had the chance to kill him. Despite his soldiers' urging, he refused to do so, for he was unwilling to raise his hand against the anointed one (*messiah*) of God. It was during a battle against the Philistines on Mount Gilboa that both Saul and Jonathan died. David then sang a beautiful lament for the two men (2 Sm 1:17-27).

The way was clear for David to become king. However, imposing his authority over the tribes of the North, still loyal to Saul, was not easy. David, of the tribe of Judah to the south, consolidated his reign in Hebron, and all the tribes of the North ultimately recognized him as king. He then had to make the strategic choice of a capital. He set his sights on Jebus, which afforded several advantages: on the one hand, the city was reputed to be impregnable, so conquering it would gain him legitimacy as a warrior; on the other hand, situated on the border between Judah and Benjamin, it would allow him to retain the support of his tribe while still opening up to the tribes of the North.

He captured the city and gave it the name Jerusalem. He decided to have the ark of the covenant moved there, transforming the city into a religious capital. During this transition, his wife Michal became angry with him for dancing half-naked before the ark. She became barren, presumably as punishment for rebuking the king. David was thus confronted with two problems: that of the future of the ark in Jerusalem and that of his posterity. It is at this moment that our text begins.

History - The Taking of Jerusalem

The covenant that God established with his people through the mediation of Moses can be compared to ancient treaties through which lords and their vassals made alliances. On one side, there is the promise of protection, on the other, an undertaking of fealty.

The Author - The Deuteronomistic History

The Book of Deuteronomy is not just the last book of the Pentateuch, relating the death of Moses. It is also the prelude to a long historic panorama, written by the same authors, which is called the "Deuteronomistic History": it stretches from the entry into the Promised Land (beginning of the Book of Joshua) up to the Babylonian exile (end of the Second Book of Kings). The story of David, in the books of Samuel, is part of this fresco.

Geography - Jerusalem

Situated between the Tyropoeon Valley to the west and the Kidron Valley to the east, the city of David would be expanded to the north, where Solomon would later construct the Temple.

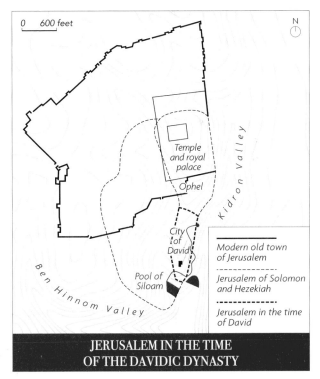

JERUSALEM IN THE TIME OF THE DAVIDIC DYNASTY

BIBLICAL TEXT (2 SAMUEL 7:1-22)

After the king had taken up residence in his house, and the LORD had given him rest from his enemies on every side, the king said to Nathan the prophet, "Here I am living in a house of cedar, but the ark of God dwells in a tent!" Nathan answered the king, "Whatever is in your heart, go and do, for the LORD is with you." But that same night the word of the LORD came to Nathan: Go and tell David my servant, Thus says the LORD: Is it you who would build me a house to dwell in? I have never dwelt in a house from the day I brought Israel up from Egypt to this day, but I have been going about in a tent or a tabernacle. As long as I have wandered about among the Israelites, did I ever say a word to any of the judges whom I commanded to shepherd my people Israel: Why have you not built me a house of cedar?

Now then, speak thus to my servant David, Thus says the LORD of hosts: I took you from the pasture, from following the flock, to become ruler over my people Israel. I was with you wherever you went, and I cut down all your enemies before you. And I will make your name like that of the greatest on earth. I will assign a place for my people Israel and I will plant them in it to dwell there; they will never again be disturbed, nor shall the wicked ever again oppress them, as they did at the beginning, and from the day when I appointed judges over my people Israel. I will give you rest from all your enemies. ∎

This excerpt is commonly known as the oracle—the prophecy—of Nathan. In it, God promises, among other things, to establish a house for David—an everlasting dynasty. The oracle is fulfilled in Jesus Christ.

⮕ Biblical Insights

God forbids David from building him a house. It is in the following generation, as we see in the First Book of Kings, that Solomon will build the Temple in fulfillment of the promise made to David.

> The king [Solomon] turned and blessed the whole assembly of Israel, while the whole assembly of Israel stood. He said: "Blessed be the LORD, the God of Israel, who with his own mouth spoke a promise to David my father and by his hand fulfilled it, saying:...I have chosen David to rule my people Israel. When David my father wished to build a house for the name of the LORD, the God of Israel."

1 Kings 8:14-17

The Letter to the Hebrews emphasizes that it was God himself who designed and built the city of Jerusalem.

> By faith Abraham...was was looking forward to the city with foundations, whose architect and maker is God.

Hebrews 11:8, 10

⮕ Fathers of the Church

Saint Augustine understood that the beneficiary of the promise made to David is not so much Solomon as Jesus, the only one whose kingdom is eternal.

> He who thinks this grand promise was fulfilled in Solomon greatly errs; for he attends to the saying, "He shall build me a house," but he does not attend to the saying, "His house shall be faithful, and his kingdom for evermore before me."

Augustine, City of God, Book XVII[9]

■■■ Moreover the LORD also declares to you that the LORD will make a house for you: when your days have been completed and you rest with your ancestors, I will raise up your offspring after you, sprung from your loins, and I will establish his kingdom. He it is who shall build a house for my name, and I will establish his royal throne forever. I will be a father to him, and he shall be a son to me. If he does wrong, I will reprove him with a human rod and with human punishments; but I will not withdraw my favor from him as I withdrew it from Saul who was before you. Your house and your kingdom are firm forever before me; your throne shall be firmly established forever. In accordance with all these words and this whole vision Nathan spoke to David.

Then King David went in and sat in the LORD's presence and said, "Who am I, Lord GOD, and what is my house, that you should have brought me so far? And yet even this is too little in your sight, Lord GOD! For you have made me a promise regarding your servant's house reaching into the future, and giving guidance to the people, Lord GOD! What more can David say to you? You know your servant, Lord GOD! For your servant's sake and as you have had at heart, you have brought about this whole magnificent disclosure to your servant. Therefore, great are you, Lord GOD! There is no one like you, no God but you, as we have always heard.

Part Three

⊃ Biblical Insights

According to the Letter to the Hebrews, the promise made to David ("I will be a father to him, and he shall be a son to me") was fully accomplished in Jesus.

> [The Son is] far superior to the angels..../ For to which of the angels did God ever say:/ "You are my son; this day I have begotten you"?/ Or again:/ "I will be a father to him, and he shall be a son to me"?

Hebrews 1:4-5

In the Annunciation to Mary, in the Gospel according to Saint Luke, the Angel Gabriel shows that Nathan's oracle is fulfilled in Jesus.

> Then the angel said to her, "Do not be afraid, Mary, for you have found favor with God. Behold, you will conceive in your womb and bear a son, and you shall name him Jesus. He will be great and will be called Son of the Most High, and the Lord God will give him the throne of David his father, and he will rule over the house of Jacob forever, and of his kingdom there will be no end."

Luke 1:30-33

⊃ Fathers of the Church

Saint Augustine maintains that in Jesus is realized the double promise of the oracle of Nathan. First, Jesus belongs to the "house of David" because he is its descendant. Second, Jesus is like the "house of God" since God resides in him.

> The son was then about to be born from whom his posterity should be continued to Christ, through whom his house should be eternal, and should also be the house of God. For it is called the house of David on account of David's race; but the selfsame is called the house of God on account of the temple of God.

Augustine, City of God, Book XVII[10]

Questions to Guide the Reading of the Text

Read the text carefully. If possible, read it aloud twice.

**LOOK AT DAVID'S
INITIAL SITUATION**
(page 98)

- What is the problem David is trying to resolve? Are his intentions straightforward? What is the ambiguity of his plan?

- Why does God intervene that same night? Does he agree with what Nathan has said to David?

**STUDY THE HISTORIC
REFERENCES GOD
SETS OUT**

- What do we learn about God's manner of living amidst his people since the flight from Egypt?

- What image does that give of God?

- Why does God mistrust what David is planning to do?

- Why does God recall David's past? How does it define the relationship between God and David?

STUDY GOD'S PLAN
(page 100)

- In the end, how does God respond to David's initiative?

- What can be said about the play on words in the term "house"?

- What do we learn about the construction of the Temple?

- What do we learn about the son of David? What will his status be in relationship to God? What can be said of his reign?

- Do you think this is just about Solomon? If not, who could it be about?

- How does David react to this oracle?

Glossary

—→ :✳: ←—

DESCENDANT *(Hebrew: zera)*: From the root word "seed," this term designates at one and the same time both "race" and "descendants." It has a strong theological significance: Isaiah would speak of the "holy seed" (Is 6:13, NIV) to refer to the members of the people who remain faithful to God.

HOUSE *(Hebrew: bayith)*: The term "house" has two accepted meanings. When used in reference to a building, it can refer to the Temple, called the "house of God." But it can also be used to speak of the household and, by extension, of descendants; this is the case in the expression "the house of David."

NAME *(Hebrew: shem)*: A person's name has a double significance. In the private realm, it reveals one's personality. In the social realm, it indicates one's fame and posterity: "I will make your name like that of the greatest on earth" (2 Sm 7:9).

SERVANT *(Hebrew: ebed)*: In addition to its basic meaning, the word "servant" is used in the Bible to denote those in the service of the Lord (patriarchs, prophets). It is particularly employed for great figures (Moses, David) and even for the whole of Israel. We find this expression in Isaiah when he refers to the "suffering servant."

Part Three

COMMENTARY

The oracle of Nathan is a major text in Biblical tradition. Indeed, it constitutes one of the vital foundations of the two most profound and frequently used themes of the Old Testament. On the one hand, the oracle orients the messianic hope: Israel is awaiting a Messiah and he will be the "son of David." On the other hand, it refutes an overly materialistic concept of the Temple.

Let's begin our reading. The situation, we will recall, leaves David with a double-edged problem: his wife is sterile, and the ark of God dwells in a tent. David takes in hand the problem with the ark and, as we will see, God responds to him in terms of David's descendants.

God sends his prophet Nathan to inform David of what he expects of him. It is through the words of the oracle that we learn of David's intention to build a house for God. But God poses a pointed question: "Is it you who would build me a house to dwell in?" God wishes to make David think about his plan. He then reminds him that God has never lived in a "house of cedar," nor asked to do so "from the day I brought Israel up from Egypt to this day." Thus an image takes shape of a nomadic God who mistrusts a sedentary life. There is, of course, a theological reason for this divine mistrust. People might be tempted to think that they can encompass God, can keep him firmly in his place in the Temple, forgetting that he is greater than any house one might care to build for him.

God counterbalances the question "Is it you who would...?" with the affirmation "I took you.... I was with you...." He thus reminds David that his entire life is in the hands of God, from the moment he took him from his flocks. The history of a God who has never wished to be confined by human concepts is followed by the history of a king who has been led by divine providence. God shows that it is he who takes the initiative.

Then comes the crucial moment of the oracle. Through a subtle play on words involving the ambiguity of the word "house," God reverses the Davidic initiative. "You want to build me a house? I'm going to build one for you." But while David is speaking of a house of cedar, God is speaking of a house of flesh and blood. And though Michal could no longer give David descendants, God promises him posterity anyway.

What God says about this posterity paints a picture of the Messiah to come. Let's take a detailed look at this.

On first reading, we learn that David will have a son to whom it will fall to construct the house of God. This concerns Solomon, who, through this oracle, obtains legitimacy to build the Temple. And, in fact, following the death of his father David, Solomon will be the builder of the Jerusalem Temple.

A question arises: why does God permit Solomon what he has denied his father? Basically, through his refusal to David, God wanted to teach a lesson about the Temple. Indeed, there will eventually be a place where God will make himself present among his people, and this place will be the Jerusalem Temple. But we must still remember that God is greater than his Temple. He makes himself present there, but he does not allow himself to be contained there. The fact that the Temple would be built on a plot of land purchased by David after he is forgiven for a sin he commits (2 Sm 24) is the sign that this Temple must be the place of man's humility before God.

Solomon takes this divine lesson to heart when, later, he dedicates the Temple: "Is God indeed to dwell on earth? If the heavens and the highest heavens cannot contain you, how much less this house which I have built!" (1 Kgs 8:27). Solomon understands that God mistrusts all man's attempts to hold him in their grasp.

A second reading is called for. The posterity of which God speaks to David will not be limited to Solomon. Indeed, God says that he will make David's successor's throne "firmly established forever." But the end of Solomon's reign was extremely unstable. We thus understand that the one spoken of in the oracle is a more distant descendant of David. In this promised son, all of biblical tradition has seen the Messiah himself, to such an extent that the expression "son of David" became a messianic title. Henceforth, a Messiah bearing the traits of a new Solomon was awaited.

The oracle announces two things. First, of this son of David, God attests: "I will be a father to him, and he shall be a son to me." This sets in place a particular filial relationship between God and the descendant of David that is called the "dynastic covenant." Second, God affirms that the throne of this descendant will be "firmly established forever." By promising faithfulness to this kingdom, God confirms that, unlike earthly kingdoms, this one will not be transitory.

Through this oracle of Nathan, we understand that the coming Messiah will have several characteristics: he will be a descendant of David; God will be a father to him; his mission will be to build the house of God, the place of the true divine presence; and his reign will be without end.

It is hardly surprising that this Old Testament passage was taken up again in the New to speak of Jesus. In fact, Christians see in Jesus the Messiah foreseen in the Scriptures, and, notably, in the oracle of Nathan. The Evangelists and other Christian writers decode the pronouncement made to David, helping us to understand it as it applies to Jesus.

Let's go back to the quotations from the Bible and the Fathers of the Church found on pages 99 and 101. We see that the Angel Gabriel, in the Annunciation to the Blessed Virgin Mary (Lk 1:31-33), describes the son she is to give birth to in the guise of the son of David. In the same way, the Letter to the Hebrews likens the Son of God to the son of David. Four centuries later, in his *City of God*, Augustine also returns to this oracle to unveil how it prophesied the coming of Jesus, the new Solomon.

It is Jesus—the Messiah, true son of David and true Son of God—about whom God is speaking when he says to David: "He it is who shall build a house for my name." And so we understand that Jesus built the house of God at the instigation of the Father: not a house made by human hands but a house that is his own flesh.

Theme - The Temple

The Jerusalem Temple was Israel's central, even unique, place of worship. Constructed by Solomon, then rebuilt after the return from exile, it occupied 35 ½ acres to the north-east of the city. In its center was found the Holy of Holies, a chamber that, until the exile, housed the ark of the covenant with the tablets of the law. It was the place of the divine presence. The sacrificial altar was also found here where the people, through the office of the priests, could offer worship to God, notably at the time of the great pilgrimage feasts.

Customs - The prophet and the king

Up until the exile, there were prophets in the royal court who advised and counseled the kings. Nathan was active at David's side to help guide his judgment. Later, Isaiah and Jeremiah would enlighten and criticize kings. The interaction between kings and prophets would never cease throughout the history of Israel, until the dissolution of royalty at the time of the exile. Biblical prophesying survived for three or four centuries beyond the exile.

Theology - The Link Between the Old and New Testaments

We've seen how much Luke borrows from the Book of Samuel (see 2 Sm 7) in the account of the Annunciation. The Old Testament is a key to understanding the New Testament, and so Christians can never read the texts of the New Testament without referring back to the Old. You cannot recognize that a promise has been fulfilled without knowing what the promise was! That captures the relationship between the two Testaments.

Spirituality - Living Stones

With the oracle of Nathan, we see that the house built by God is a house of "living stones." In the New Testament, the expression is taken up again by the Apostle Peter to speak of the Church: "Like living stones, let yourselves be built into a spiritual house" (1 Pt 2:5). The Christian is aware that, along with all other baptized persons, he is the dwelling-house of God.

LECTIO DIVINA

For a prayerful reading related to the oracle of Nathan, here are some verses from the First Book of Kings in which Solomon prays to God following the construction of the Temple.

Solomon stood before the altar of the LORD in the presence of the whole assembly of Israel, and stretching forth his hands toward heaven, he said… "And now, LORD, God of Israel, keep toward your servant, David my father, what you promised:…

"Is God indeed to dwell on earth? If the heavens and the highest heavens cannot contain you, how much less this house which I have built! Regard kindly the prayer and petition of your servant, LORD, my God, and listen to the cry of supplication which I, your servant, utter before you this day. May your eyes be open night and day toward this house, the place of which you said, My name shall be there; listen to the prayer your servant makes toward this place."

1 Kings 8:22-23a, 25a, 27-29

A PSALM FOR MEDITATION

The LORD swore an oath to David in truth,
he will never turn back from it:
"Your own offspring I will set upon your throne.
If your sons observe my covenant,
and my decrees I shall teach them,
Their sons, in turn,
shall sit forever on your throne."
Yes, the LORD has chosen Zion,
desired it for a dwelling:
"This is my resting place forever;
here I will dwell, for I desire it.
I will bless Zion with provisions;
its poor I will fill with bread.
I will clothe its priests with salvation;
its devout shall shout for joy.
There I will make a horn sprout for David;
I will set a lamp for my anointed.
His foes I will clothe with shame,
but on him his crown shall shine."

Psalm 132:11-18

Part Three

RECOGNIZING THE RISEN ONE
The Disciples of Emmaus
(Luke 24:13-35)

Literary context - The Stories of the Resurrection

At the end of their accounts, the four Evangelists recount the Passion and Resurrection of Jesus. First they narrate with precision his going up to his Death: his last days in Jerusalem, his Last Supper with the disciples, and his praying and arrest in the garden of Gethsemane. Then his double trial before the high priests and the Roman proconsul, Pilate, takes place. Following his condemnation, Jesus carries his cross to the place of his execution. He dies on Friday afternoon around three o'clock.

The Passion stories are very similar from one Gospel to another, but each Evangelist sets out the stories related to the Resurrection in his own way. From the discovery of the empty tomb to the sending out of the Apostles on their mission following the Risen Jesus' manifestations to the disciples, Matthew, Mark, Luke, and John select and organize their last chapters as the culmination of their works.

At the beginning of his last chapter, Luke relates the discovery of the empty tomb by the women; he positions this story as a continuation of the previous chapter, which had ended with the moment when the women leave the tomb on Friday:

The women who had come from Galilee with him followed behind, and when they had seen the tomb and the way in which his body was laid in it, they returned and prepared spices and perfumed oils. Then they rested on the sabbath according to the commandment.

Luke 23:55-56

But at daybreak on the first day of the week they took the spices they had prepared and went to the tomb. They found the stone rolled away from the tomb; but when they entered, they did not find the body of the Lord Jesus.

Luke 24:1-3

Luke insists on the continuity of their witness. These are the same women who had seen the tomb with the corpse and who now discover it empty. This is in no way proof of the Resurrection, but it is a fact that will give rise to speculation.

From that point, Luke relates three successive encounters in which the empty tomb is justified by the fact that Jesus is Risen. They all take place on Sunday, when the presence of Jesus becomes more and more of a reality: at the tomb, Jesus is absent but is declared alive by the two men in dazzling garments (Lk 24:1-12). On the road to Emmaus, Jesus is there, but he is only recognized at the moment he vanishes (Lk 24:13-35). In Jerusalem, Jesus manifests himself in visible form in the midst of the Apostles and, once recognized, he leaves them (Lk 24:36-51). So it is within the framework of the recognition of the Risen One that the Emmaus episode we are now studying plays out.

History - The Historical Authenticity of the Resurrection

Nothing in the Gospels proves the historical authenticity of the Resurrection. The four Gospels insist on the reality of the fact, however, affirming that Jesus was not a ghost: the disciples had touched him. According to the Gospels, the Resurrection is not a figment of the Apostles' imagination or an ideological reconstruction by the first community. If faith in the Resurrection of Jesus is not founded on proof, it is based on the witness of the first disciples, the Evangelists among them, who stated that he was alive.

The Author - Luke, the Companion of Paul

A disciple of Saint Paul, Luke was probably the only one of the four Evangelists not to have known Jesus. In writing his Gospel, he explains that he had recourse to the eyewitnesses (Lk 1:1-4). An astute scholar of Scripture, he composed his Gospel according to the canons of Hellenistic literature. His work also includes a second component, the Acts of the Apostles.

Geography - The Apparitions

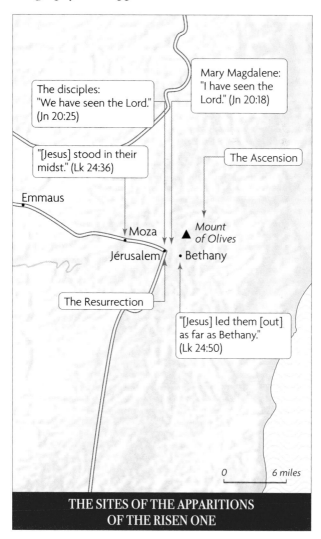

The disciples:
"We have seen the Lord."
(Jn 20:25)

Mary Magdalene:
"I have seen the
Lord." (Jn 20:18)

"[Jesus] stood in their
midst." (Lk 24:36)

The Ascension

Emmaus

Moza

▲ Mount
of Olives

Jérusalem

• Bethany

The Resurrection

"[Jesus] led them [out]
as far as Bethany."
(Lk 24:50)

0   6 miles

**THE SITES OF THE APPARITIONS
OF THE RISEN ONE**

BIBLICAL TEXT (LUKE 24:13-35)

Now that very day two of them were going to a village seven miles from Jerusalem called Emmaus, and they were conversing about all the things that had occurred. And it happened that while they were conversing and debating, Jesus himself drew near and walked with them, but their eyes were prevented from recognizing him. He asked them, "What are you discussing as you walk along?" They stopped, looking downcast. One of them, named Cleopas, said to him in reply, "Are you the only visitor to Jerusalem who does not know of the things that have taken place there in these days?" And he replied to them, "What sort of things?" They said to him, "The things that happened to Jesus the Nazarene, who was a prophet mighty in deed and word before God and all the people, how our chief priests and rulers both handed him over to a sentence of death and crucified him. But we were hoping that he would be the one to redeem Israel; and besides all this, it is now the third day since this took place. Some women from our group, however, have astounded us: they were at the tomb early in the morning and did not find his body; they came back and reported that they had indeed seen a vision of angels who announced that he was alive. Then some of those with us went to the tomb and found things just as the women had described, but him they did not see." ■■■

➲ Biblical Insights

Jesus chose not to make himself immediately identifiable to the disciples on the way to Emmaus; he has them make a spiritual journey. This recalls the story of Joseph, sold as a slave by his jealous brothers. When they meet him again in Egypt, Joseph, unrecognizable in his position as Pharaoh's steward, progressively leads his brothers to recognize him.

> He recognized them as soon as he saw them. But he concealed his own identity from them and spoke harshly to them. "Where do you come from?" he asked them. They answered, "From the land of Canaan, to buy food."...
>
> Joseph recognized his brothers, although they did not recognize him.

Genesis 42:7-8

The Emmaus episode is summed up in the finale of the Gospel of Mark, the only other account to mention this encounter.

> After this he appeared in another form to two of them walking along on their way to the country. They returned and told the others; but they did not believe them either.

Mark 16:12-13

➲ Fathers of the Church

Saint Augustine considers the despair of the two disciples. They hadn't believed what Jesus had foretold, and now he brings them to their senses.

> What he had foretold came to pass. And those who had heard him did not believe it. "It is now the third day since this took place. But we were hoping that he would be the one to redeem Israel...." You hoped, and now you despair? You have fallen from the great heights of your hope. He who walks with you will raise you up again.

Saint Augustine, Easter Sermon[11]

■■■ And he said to them, "Oh, how foolish you are! How slow of heart to believe all that the prophets spoke! Was it not necessary that the Messiah should suffer these things and enter into his glory?" Then beginning with Moses and all the prophets, he interpreted to them what referred to him in all the scriptures. As they approached the village to which they were going, he gave the impression that he was going on farther. But they urged him, "Stay with us, for it is nearly evening and the day is almost over." So he went in to stay with them. And it happened that, while he was with them at table, he took bread, said the blessing, broke it, and gave it to them. With that their eyes were opened and they recognized him, but he vanished from their sight. Then they said to each other, "Were not our hearts burning [within us] while he spoke to us on the way and opened the scriptures to us?" So they set out at once and returned to Jerusalem where they found gathered together the eleven and those with them who were saying, "The Lord has truly been raised and has appeared to Simon!" Then the two recounted what had taken place on the way and how he was made known to them in the breaking of the bread.

➲ Biblical Insights

In his epistle, Peter recalls that he who announces the salvation of God is a prophet.

> Concerning this salvation, prophets who prophesied about the grace that was to be yours searched and investigated it.

1 Peter 1:10

In the breaking of the bread before the two disciples, Jesus repeats the gesture he used at the multiplication of the loaves. It is perhaps because of this that the disciples recognize Jesus in this act.

> Then taking the five loaves and the two fish, and looking up to heaven, [Jesus] said the blessing over them, broke them, and gave them to the disciples to set before the crowd.

Luke 9:16

➲ Fathers of the Church

Melito of Sardis insists that Jesus' journey of suffering is consistent with its foretelling in Scripture.

> Indeed, the Lord prearranged his own sufferings in the patriarchs, and in the prophets, and in the whole people of God, giving his sanction to them through the law and the prophets. For that which was to exist in a new and grandiose fashion was pre-planned long in advance, in order that when it should come into existence one might attain to faith, just because it had been predicted long in advance.

Melito of Sardis, On Easter[12]

Part Three

Questions to Guide the Reading of the Text

Read the text carefully. If possible, read it aloud twice.

STUDY JESUS' ENCOUNTER WITH THE TWO DISCIPLES (page 116)

• What is the geographical setting of this episode? Do you think it is important?

• Unlike the disciples, the reader knows that it's Jesus whom they are meeting. What does that imply?

• Why do you think Jesus doesn't make himself known right away?

STUDY THE TWO DISCIPLES' RESPONSE

• Why do you think Luke specifies the name of Cleopas?

• Why does Jesus have the disciples recount what had happened? What are the events in his life related by the two disciples?

• What can be said about their expectations? About their disappointments?

STUDY JESUS' REACTION (page 118)

• Why does Jesus begin with the Scriptures? How does he interpret them?

• Why do you think Luke doesn't recount this teaching?

• What will we learn of the effect this teaching had on the disciples? Why aren't we told here?

STUDY THE MEAL AT EMMAUS

• Why does Jesus give the impression that he's going farther on? Is he toying with the two disciples?

• What causes the disciples to recognize Jesus? Why do you think Jesus vanishes?

• What can explain the disciples' immediate reaction? Why do they return to Jerusalem?

Glossary

—— ➤ ☀ ◄ ——

GLORY *(Greek: doxa)*: Jesus announces that he must suffer before entering into his "glory" (Lk 24:26). This term comes from the Old Testament and refers to the plenitude of the divine presence and splendor. For Luke, Jesus reenters into his glory at the moment of the Ascension.

HIGH PRIESTS *(Greek: archiereis)*: The high priests were in charge of the practice of worship in the Jerusalem Temple. They constituted a few very powerful families, akin to the Sadducees. In the time of Jesus, the high priest was selected on a hereditary basis and was recognized by the people and by Rome as the head of the Jewish nation.

INTERPRET *(Greek: diermèneuô)*: One of the important roles of the Jewish rabbi is to reveal the meaning of Scripture. The word "hermeneutic" (that is, the interpretation of biblical texts) derives from this Greek term.

IT IS NECESSARY *(Greek: dei)*: Jesus often uses these words to express the necessity of his Passion. It has less to do with a legal obligation than an obligation of love freely assumed, linked to Scripture.

SCRIPTURES *(Greek: graphaï)*: "Scriptures" refers to all of the written texts that are part of the religious heritage of Israel. For the authors of the New Testament, the term is used to refer to what would be called the Old Testament: the law, the prophets, and other texts.

COMMENTARY

The encounter of the Risen Jesus with the two disciples on the road to Emmaus constitutes, without contest, some of the most beautiful pages of the Gospels. On the very day of the Resurrection, Jesus approaches these two. Only one—Cleopas—is named, leaving the reader the possibility of identifying with the second.

The topographical route they take from Jerusalem to Emmaus is in fact a spiritual journey. By coming to meet them, then engaging them in conversation without making himself known, Jesus takes charge of their journey: at first, their eyes are prevented from recognizing him; in the end, "their eyes were opened and they recognized him."

We might wonder why Jesus waits such a long time—a day's journey—before revealing his identity. The reader knows from the start that it's him: why doesn't Jesus tell the two disciples? Undoubtedly because it's not a question of simple physical recognition. This is precisely why the reader knows Jesus' identity: we must not be preoccupied with wondering if it's about him—we already know; rather, we must understand the manner in which Jesus wishes to make himself known. It is also for this reason that Jesus can vanish from before the disciples' eyes when they recognize him: it's no longer the physical presence that counts.

Let's now look at how Jesus goes about leading the two. He opens the conversation by joining in the disciples' discussion. He first urges them to recount their story. They then give a gripping summary of the whole event of "Jesus the Nazarene."

Beginning by echoing the stories of the birth ("Jesus the Nazarene"), they evoke Jesus' public ministry ("a prophet mighty in deed and word before God and all the people"), then the events of the Passion ("how our chief priests and rulers both handed him over to a sentence of death and crucified him"). Finally, they allude to what happened that same morning, with the visit of the women to the tomb and the apostles' skeptical confirmation of things.

This magnificent summation is certainly a brilliant stroke by Luke: like a great Hellenistic author, he tops off his work with a final synthesis. This is above all the moment to note that the two disciples are at a dead end in their understanding of the facts: "We were hoping that he would be the one to redeem Israel.... Some of those with us went to the tomb and found things just as the women had described, but him they did not see." In their brilliant summary, the disciples forget to mention that Jesus had foretold his Death and Resurrection. Through this omission, they are missing the key to a proper interpretation!

Note that Jesus could have made himself known at this precise moment. But he prefers to launch into a great explanatory biblical lesson. It's not physical recognition that's most important for Jesus, but the congruity between his life and the Scriptures. Of course, the reader doesn't know what Jesus said, nor how he went about interpreting the Old Testament. But we know that an understanding of Scripture is necessary in order to recognize the Risen One. One might have in mind these words attributed to Abraham at the end of the parable of Lazarus: "If they will not listen to Moses and the prophets, neither will they be persuaded if someone should rise from the dead" (Lk 16:31).

The time between first meeting Jesus and recognizing him is a time set aside for the interior transformation of the two disciples. It's this time for the explanation of the Scriptures that the two disciples will say revitalized them. For, indeed, what do they remember when a few moments later Jesus vanishes from before their eyes? That their hearts had been burning when he opened up the Scriptures to them. To recognize Jesus with their hearts and not just with their eyes is above all a question of understanding what he underwent in light of the Scriptures.

Jesus did not make himself immediately known to the disciples because he wanted to bring them beyond mere physical recognition. He made them grasp that, though absent from our physical sight, Jesus would always be present. After the breaking of the bread, his disappearance doesn't equate to his absence. And that's why the fact of no longer seeing Jesus arouses no regret or sadness in the disciples. It doesn't even bother them. On the contrary, they would henceforth have another form of presence.

Let us now look at the reader's place in the story. At the start, we know more than the two disciples, since we know that this is Jesus. However, along the way we feel frustration, for we're not present for Jesus' biblical explanations. We may wonder why Luke doesn't relate this teaching that so enlightened the two disciples and made their hearts burn. But we will indeed end up profiting from Jesus' teaching—we need simply await Luke's second volume: the Acts of the Apostles. There we will find the interpretation of the Scriptures given by Jesus, not in his words but in those of the Apostles, for Jesus entrusted to his Church the task of continuing to spread his teaching.

The end of our story underscores the importance of the Apostles' authority. Although the two disciples recognized Jesus in the breaking of the bread, they understood, on their return to Jerusalem, that it was up to the Apostles to confirm the authenticity of their encounter: "The Lord has truly been raised!"

And so the story of Emmaus constitutes a bridge for the contemporary reader. It sums up the past and the future at the same time: the past, because it summarizes all of Scripture and all of Jesus' ministry, and demonstrates the consistency between the event of Jesus Christ and the Old Testament; the future, because it also illuminates the path of all humanity. The Risen One utterly transforms the life of the disciple who recognizes him, not with physical eyes, but through a recognition of the heart. This is why the Christian today does not need the physical presence of Jesus in order to believe in him. Each of us is called to encounter the living Jesus along the road, present through his Church, which continues to spread his word and celebrate the breaking of the bread.

Theme - The Resurrection

Faith in the resurrection of the dead had already figured among Judaic beliefs for several centuries before Jesus. The crossing of the Red Sea itself is understood as a prophecy of resurrection. The prophets Isaiah, Ezekiel, and Daniel wrote many prophecies that make clear the conviction that God is stronger than bodily death. In the New Testament, the Gospels and the letters of Paul attest to the faith of the nascent Church, not only in the bodily Resurrection of Jesus, but in that of humanity as well, freed from death by Jesus.

Customs - Pilgrimage to Jerusalem

The Jerusalem Temple was the only authorized place of worship in Judaism. On the occasion of the three great feasts (Passover, Pentecost, and the feast of Tabernacles or Booths), numerous pilgrims from throughout the country and the diaspora converged on the Holy City. In his childhood, Jesus himself went there for the great feasts (Lk 2:41). It's possible that the disciples of Emmaus were among these pilgrims to Jerusalem for the Passover. The Ethiopian eunuch we will read about in the Lectio Divina feature (page 128) had "come to Jerusalem to worship," and so might also have been a pilgrim for one of the great feasts.

Theology - Apostolic Confirmation

The encounter of the two disciples with the Risen One is not enough. It is necessary that it be authenticated by the Apostles, who represent the Church. One of the Church's roles is to help the faithful evaluate their spiritual experiences. The Church was instituted by Jesus to be the steward of his message, and it is up to her to discern whether the words or deeds of a person are in conformity with the Gospel.

Spirituality - Recognition of the Heart

The spiritual life involves a willingness to renounce the longing for the perceptible presence of God (cf. Dt 5:8: "You shall not carve idols for yourselves in the shape of anything in the sky above"). It is not with our physical eyes or the touch of our hands that we grasp God. We encounter God, we encounter the Risen Jesus, through the recognition of the heart. This happens through prayer, but also through confidence in the witnesses whom God chose.

LECTIO DIVINA

For a meditative reading related to the episode at Emmaus, here are some verses about Philip's meeting with the Ethiopian court official, from the Acts of the Apostles:

[Philip] got up and set out. Now there was an Ethiopian eunuch, a court official of the Candace, that is, the queen of the Ethiopians, in charge of her entire treasury, who had come to Jerusalem to worship, and was returning home. Seated in his chariot, he was reading the prophet Isaiah. The Spirit said to Philip, "Go and join up with that chariot." Philip ran up and heard him reading Isaiah the prophet and said, "Do you understand what you are reading?" He replied, "How can I, unless someone instructs me?" So he invited Philip to get in and sit with him.... Then Philip opened his mouth and, beginning with this scripture passage, he proclaimed Jesus to him.

Acts of the Apostles 8:27-31, 35

A PSALM FOR MEDITATION

I wait for the LORD,
who bends down to me and hears my cry,
Draws me up from the pit of destruction,
out of the muddy clay,
Sets my feet upon rock,
steadies my steps,
And puts a new song in my mouth,
a hymn to our God.
Many shall look on in fear
and they shall trust in the Lord.
Blessed the man who sets
his security in the LORD,
who turns not to the arrogant
or to those who stray after falsehood.
You, yes you, O LORD, my God,
have done many wondrous deeds!
And in your plans for us
there is none to equal you.
Should I wish to declare or tell them,
too many are they to recount.

Psalm 40:2-6

Part Three

– CONCLUSION –

Now I am reminding you, brothers, of the gospel I preached
to you, which you indeed received and in which you also
stand. Through it you are also being saved, if you hold
fast to the word I preached to you, unless you believed in
vain. For I handed on to you as of first importance what
I also received: that Christ died for our sins in accordance
with the scriptures; that he was buried; that he was raised
on the third day in accordance with the scriptures; that
he appeared to Cephas, then to the Twelve. After that, he
appeared to more than five hundred brothers at once, most
of whom are still living, though some have fallen asleep.
After that he appeared to James, then to all the apostles.
Last of all, as to one born abnormally, he appeared to me.

1 Corinthians 15:1-8

Thus does Saint Paul address the inhabitants of Corinth.
Paul did not know Jesus during the time of Jesus' ministry on
earth. A Jew by birth, training, and conviction, Paul converted
to Christ when, on the road to Damascus to arrest followers
of "the Way," that is, disciples of Christ, he encountered a
blinding light, fell to the ground, and heard Jesus ask him: "Why
are you persecuting me?" Paul then, too, became a follower
of the Way, a man who, like the Apostles, maintained that
Jesus is the Messiah of Israel (see Acts 9:1-28). He is called the
Apostle to the Gentiles because he was the first to receive
the mission to carry the Gospel to the entire world.

A Jew steeped in the Old Testament and announcing the
Resurrection of Christ to the world: what better guide could
we have to sum up the entirety of our journey of biblical
discovery?

Like Moses, Paul was chosen and prepared to announce salvation among his brethren (see text no. 1 on the birth of Moses, pages 19-35). Like Jesus, he performed acts of power, restoring life to those who had lost it (see text no. 2 on the double miracle of Jesus, pages 36-56). He was a man of the law, a Pharisee, the son of Pharisees (see text no. 3 on the Decalogue, pages 57-73), who followed the law through to its fulfillment: the love between God and humanity (see text no. 4 on the encounter of Jesus and the Samaritan woman, pages 74-94). Finally, he who understood that the presence of God could not be circumscribed in a Temple made by human hands (see text no. 5 on the oracle of Nathan, pages 95-111), recognized that the Risen Jesus was well and truly the One awaited in the Old Testament (like the disciples of Emmaus in text no. 6, pages 112-129): Paul's life was utterly transformed by his encounter with Jesus Christ, for he experienced the fulfillment of Scripture. For him, a biblical journey became a life journey.

Through these few pages, my intention has been to allow everyone to savor the meaning of biblical literature. As we've seen, it is difficult to advance in reading the Bible without being captivated by its central character: Jesus Christ. The echo between the Old and New Testaments—the authentic coherence between Old and New—reflects the coherence of our own existence, united with God and illuminated by the light of Jesus Christ.

How to proceed from here? Many possibilities are open to you. You can of course immerse yourself in the Bible (preferably a Catholic edition) and read a few passages regularly.

You could begin with the Book of Genesis, the two Books of Samuel, one of the four Gospels, or the Acts of the Apostles. You could also attend courses—either online or in your diocese—or Bible studies, as well as read some of the many good Catholic books about the Bible on the market today. It's also helpful to get together with others simply to read the Bible.

For a daily encounter with the Word of God in the liturgy, you could subscribe to the monthly magazine MAGNIFICAT. To discover the Gospels and the Letters of Saint Paul day by day, please refer to the *Praying With...* series also published by MAGNIFICAT (www.magnificat.com).

From a methodological point of view, you can safely apply the method we have used here in these six successive texts: being attentive to the letter of the text in order to bring out its deep meaning. A prayerful reading will certainly aid a more personal internalization and an authentic encounter with Jesus. Reading in a group or with an instructor will foster a more exact and engaging understanding of the text.

May you now set off on the adventure of the Bible, opening your heart and mind to the Lord without fear!

Notes

1. Origen, *Homilies on Genesis and Exodus*, The Fathers of the Church 71, tr. Ronald E. Heine. Washington, D.C.: Catholic University of America Press, 1981.

2. Migne, *Patrologia Graeca* 69, tr. Janet Chevrier.

3. Hilary of Poitiers, *Commentary on Matthew*, The Fathers of the Church 125, tr. D.H. Williams. Washington, D.C.: Catholic University of America Press, 2012.

4. *Sources Chrétiennes* 494, tr. Janet Chevrier.

5. *Sources Chrétiennes* 271, tr. Janet Chevrier.

6. Origen, *Homilies on Genesis and Exodus*.

7. *Nicene and Post-Nicene Fathers*, The Early Church Fathers 14, First Series, ed. Philip Schaff et al., tr. Charles Marriott. Buffalo, N.Y.: Christian Literature Publishing Co., 1889. Revised and edited for *New Advent* by Kevin Knight. First sentence translated by Janet Chevrier.

8. Cyril of Alexandria, *Commentary on John,* Ancient Christian Texts 1, ed. Joel C. Elowsky, tr. David R. Maxwell. Downers Grove, Ill: InterVarsity Press, 2013.

9. *Nicene and Post-Nicene Fathers*, The Early Church Fathers 2, First Series, ed. Philip Schaff et al., tr. Marcus Dods. Buffalo, N.Y.: Christian Literature Publishing Co., 1887. Revised and edited for *New Advent* by Kevin Knight.

10. Ibid.

11. *Sources Chrétiennes* 116, tr. Janet Chevrier.

12. *Sources Chrétiennes* 126, http://www.kerux.com/doc/0401A1.asp.

Publisher: Pierre-Marie Dumont
Vice President, Publishing: Romain Lizé

Author: Rev. Jean-Philippe Fabre
Translator: Janet Chevrier
Proofreader: Claire Gilligan
Layout and cover: Gauthier Delauné
Iconography: Isabelle Mascaras
Production: Pascale van de Walle, Gwendoline da Rocha
Cover: *Education of the Virgin*, Georges De La Tour (1593-1652, Workshop of),
Louvre Museum, Paris, France. © Photo Josse / Leemage.

Printed by Imprimerie Marquis, Canada, May 2017
Edition number: MGN17019
ISBN: 978-1-941709-42-9

PRAYING WITH...
A Day-by-Day Series

— FATHER PETER JOHN CAMERON, O.P. —
editor-in-chief of MAGNIFICAT

**Powerful page-a-day Scripture reflections
to lead you through each Gospel
or the letters of Saint Paul within a year**

A PSALTER FOR COUPLES
Praying the Psalms with the One You Love

— PIERRE-MARIE DUMONT —
founder of MAGNIFICAT

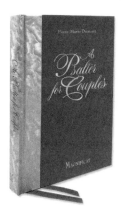

**An inspiring collection
of 70 psalms and prayers
to pray together, united as
one heart and one soul**

US $19.95

Gold and red semi-leather cover
5 x 7 in. – 264 pages
Two satin ribbons – Gilded edges

LOVE IN MARRIAGE
On living and growing in love

— POPE FRANCIS —

**Chapter 4 of the pope's
Apostolic Exhortation**
Amoris Laetitia
with questions for reflection

US $5.99

Softcover – 4.5 x 6.7 in. – 128 pages
Also available as an eBook

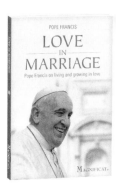

As low as $1.99 – Bulk prices available at www.loveinmarriage.org

ORDER FORM

Order online at www.magnificat.com
or complete the order form below

BOOK	PER COPY	QTY	TOTAL
SAINT PAUL	US $9.95	......	....
SAINT MATTHEW'S GOSPEL	US $9.95	......	....
SAINT MARK'S GOSPEL	US $9.95	......	....
SAINT LUKE'S GOSPEL	US $9.95	......	....
SAINT JOHN'S GOSPEL	US $9.95	......	....
A PSALTER FOR COUPLES	US $19.95	......	....
LOVE IN MARRIAGE	US $5.99	......	....
+ SHIPPING AND HANDLING (see chart below)			....
If you live in Colorado or New York, please include sales tax			
		TOTAL = US $	....

Only available in the United States and Canada.

SHIPPING AND HANDLING		
PER ORDER	USA	CANADA
Up to US $7.99	US $1	US $2
US $8 to US $15.99	US $2	US $4
US $16 to US $49.99	US $5	US $10
US $50 to US $99.99	US $8	US $16
US $100 to US $299.99	US $16	US $32
US $300 or more	6% of the order	9% of the order

MY INFORMATION

|_____| |_____|

TITLE   FIRST NAME

|_____|

LAST NAME

|_____|

ADDRESS

|_____|

|_____| |_____| |_____|

CITY   STATE   ZIP / POSTCODE

|_____| |_____| |_____| |_____|

COUNTRY   PHONE

METHOD OF PAYMENT

❑ CHECK ENCLOSED (payable to Magnificat, US $ only) *All checks must be drawn on a US bank.*

❑ MASTERCARD   ❑ VISA   ❑ DISCOVER

No. |_____| |_____| |_____| |_____|

EXPIRATION DATE |_____|/|_____| SECURITY CODE |_____|

NAME ON CARD _____

SIGNATURE

Please mail this completed order card with payment to
Magnificat-BCR
1331 Red Cedar Circle – Fort Collins, CO 80524
call 1-970-416-6670
or fax 1-970-224-1824
or email bookstore@magnificat.com
or visit www.magnificat.com/bookstore

If you are uplifted by your journey with *Breaking Open the Bible*...walk with MAGNIFICAT all year long!

*C*ontinue to be accompanied in your daily encounter with Jesus, his Blessed Mother, and his Church.

*R*ead more personal accounts of lives for ever changed in Christ.

*E*nter more fully into the prayer of the Church and her liturgical rhythm.

*P*articipate more fervently at Mass.

MAGNIFICAT has inspired the prayer
lives of millions all over the world....

Why not yours?

Today, when I gave Jim the MAGNIFICAT, he looked at me and said, "Lisa, aside from bringing me the Eucharist, of all the things you've given me and have done for me, sharing the MAGNIFICAT is the best gift you've given me."
                                                      Lisa S.

Mom LOVES MAGNIFICAT! I just wanted to tell you how much your publication has instantly become part of her personal spiritual reawakening. She is advanced in age, and had stopped attending Mass altogether for years due to her physical limitations and discomfort, but of late she is attending daily with me!
                                                      Bill B.

MAGNIFICAT continues to be my first recommendation for people who seek a daily Mass resource and introduction into the practice of Morning and Evening Prayer.   Father Matthew

Visit www.magnificat.com
and subscribe today.

MAGNIFICAT®
Your prayer life will never be the same!

DAILY MASS ❧ PRAYERS ❧ MEDITATIONS
SAINTS' LIVES ❧ STORIES OF FAITH
ART COMMENTARIES ❧ AND MORE!

Become part of the growing MAGNIFICAT family
and save up to 50% off the cover price!

USA	6 MONTHS	1 YEAR	2 YEARS	4 YEARS
Regular Edition (4.5 x 6.7 in.)	☐ **$24.95** $4.16 / month	☐ **$44.95** $3.75 / month	☐ **$79.95** $3.33 / month	☐ **$139.95** $2.92 / month
Large Print Edition (5 x 7.7 in.) 30% larger	☐ **$34.95** $5.83 / month	☐ **$64.95** $5.41 / month	☐ **$119** $4.96 / month	☐ **$236** $4.92 / month

Subscribers also have FREE ACCESS to our online and app editions.

A subscription offers 13 issues a year (one per month and a special issue for Holy Week). This edition uses the official U.S. New American Bible Lectionary.

For subscriptions in other countries and for our other English edition (UK, Ireland, Australia, etc.), please visit www.magnificat.com.

Please allow 4-6 weeks from receipt of order for delivery of your first issue.

PLEASE RETURN THIS SUBSCRIPTION FORM TO

MAGNIFICAT
PO Box 822 – Yonkers, NY 10702

Or fax 1-914-969-6446
Or call 1-866-273-5215
Or visit www.magnificat.com

MAGNIFICAT is also available in Spanish
please visit www.magnificat.com

MY INFORMATION

TITLE _____   FIRST NAME _____

LAST NAME _____

ADDRESS _____

ADDRESS _____

CITY _____   STATE _____

ZIP _____   COUNTRY _____

PHONE NUMBER _____   YEAR OF BIRTH _____

EMAIL _____

METHOD OF PAYMENT

❑ **CHECK ENCLOSED** (CHECK PAYABLE TO MAGNIFICAT, US $ ONLY)

❑ VISA   ❑ MASTERCARD   ❑ DISCOVER   ❑ AMEX

CARD No. _____

EXPIRATION DATE ____/____   SECURITY CODE _____

SIGNATURE _____

Mailing list: We occasionally make our list available to other companies whose products or services might interest you. If you would prefer not to be included, please let us know via mail, by emailing magnificat@magnificat.com, or by checking this box ❑.